T0079729

Luďa Klusáková et al.

Small Towns in Europe in the 20th and 21st Centuries
Heritage and Development Strategies

KAROLINUM PRESS
PRAGUE, 2017

KAROLINUM PRESS
Karolinum Press is a publishing department of Charles University
Ovocný trh 560/5, 116 36 Prague 1, Czech Republic
www.karolinum.cz
© Karolinum Press, 2017
Editorial matter, selection and preface © Luďa Klusáková, 2017
Remaining chapters © Respective authors, 2017
Photography © Respective authors
Language supervision by Peter Kirk Jensen
Layout by Jan Šerých
Set and printed in the Czech Republic by Karolinum Press
First edition

A catalogue record for this book is available from the National Library
of the Czech Republic.

The publication was supported by the Research Framework of Charles University
PROGRES Q09 – History – Key for the Understanding of the Global World.

ISBN 978-80-246-3645-0
ISBN 978-80-246-3656-6 (pdf)

The original manuscript was reviewed by Professor Dobrinka Parusheva
(Plovdiv University, Institute of Balkan Studies, Sofia) and Associate Professor
Zdeněk Uherek (The Institute of Ethnology of the Czech Academy of Sciences,
Prague).

Contents

Preface
Luďa Klusáková   7

Small Towns as a European Cultural Heritage. Introduction
Luďa Klusáková and Marie-Vic Ozouf-Marignier   11

Performing the Past: Identity, Civic Culture and Historical Pageants
in Twentieth-Century English Small Towns
Angela Bartie, Linda Fleming, Mark Freeman, Tom Hulme and Paul Readman   24

"The architectural rhythm of a small town ... is very familiar to us."
A Small Town as an Aesthetic Ideal of the Twentieth Century
Martin Horáček   52

Strategies of Manufacturing the Tourist Experience in a Small Town:
Local Community and Symbolic Construction in Myshkin
Greg Yudin and Yulia Koloshenko   74

Urban Cores and Urban Identity: Appropriating and Rejecting
a City's History. The Case of Rethymno
Olga Moatsou   97

Miraculous Equilibrium. Keys for a Sustainable Network of Small
South Iberian Cities
Blanca Del Espino Hidalgo   115

Concluding remarks
Luďa Klusáková and Marie-Vic Ozouf-Marignier   140

Bibliography   142
Note on Authors   156

Preface
Ľuďa Klusáková

Our book presents the results of research carried out by scholars of various disciplines (historians, sociologists, architects, and art specialists) and is focussed on the status of contemporary small towns in several European countries. The authors study how town managers and others try to make the best of the not very favourable situation of being a relatively unimportant, peripheral area dependent on a large, influential urban conglomerate. In addition, they examine how architects and planners view the organization of space in a small town.

Small towns, overshadowed by big cities and metropolises, remain a distinct feature of European settlement. While large urban sprawls, with their concomitant suburban malls, highways, skyscrapers, and the like, may seem to lack individuality when compared globally, small towns, on the contrary, retain specific spatial organization, forms of social life, including face to face contact, and engender variety and different regional types.

Which towns qualify as small towns? In scholarly discourse, small towns are classified as those that maintain their traditions and memory, as opposed to large towns where the focus is on the future with, in consequence, a progressive loss of memory. The first are categorized as societies of memory, the second as societies of change.[1] Such an interpretation, however, suggests a rather gloomy prognosis for the future of small towns.

When the co-authors of the book met at a conference of the European Association for Urban History in Lisbon in 2014, they found that their

---

1 Mariusz Zemło quoting Danielle Hervieu-Léger in "Tradycjonalizm małego miasta." In *Małe Miasta. Historia i współczesność* ["Small Town's Traditionalism." In *Small Towns. History and Present Times*], edited by Mariusz Zemło and Przemysław Czyżewski (Supraśl 2001), 133–134.

research had a common denominator: an interest in the social function of small towns. The problem of defining what constitutes a small town is touched on only when choosing examples but the point is not laboured. The case studies discuss the interconnection between cultural heritage and its commodification in various situations.

What were the issues that confronted small towns in various parts of Europe in the 20th and 21st centuries? In five chapters the authors present their findings and their selection of illustrative cases. A shared feature in all is a questioning of the role of history and how it is displayed and exploited, at times even manipulated. Indeed, heritage appears to be an underlying characteristic in all the chapters.

A team of British historians, Angela Bartie, Linda Fleming, Mark Freeman, Tom Hulme and Paul Readman, in the chapter entitled "Performing the Past: Identity, Civic Culture and Historical Pageants in Twentieth-Century Small Towns," discuss the modifications and changes made to traditional pageants – shows depicting historical scenes – which used to be very popular in England. The chapter is a revealing and incisive analysis of local patriotism that resonates with the following one on Myshkin, which focusses on the building of a local community through constructing/reconstructing history and the setting up of regular town-wide events.

The authors, Greg Yudin and Yulia Koloshenko, both specialists in economic sociology, examine the process of the "touristification" of a previously not very interesting provincial Russian town, which had no particular historical monuments and, many would say, no real potential for becoming a tourist destination. In their chapter, "Strategies of manufacturing tourist experience in a small town," they discuss the success story of Myshkin, where the struggle over town/village status has been crucial for local identity.

The following two chapters, on the other hand, were written by historians of architecture. They deal with regional examples from the southern part of Europe. In "Urban Cores and Urban Identity: Appropriating and Rejecting a City's History," Olga Moatsou looks at small towns in Greece, particularly Rhetymno on the island of Crete. Setting the case study in the context of the national urban network, the author stresses the pertinence of disputes concerning the administrative classification of small towns and their borders in terms of political organization, urban planning and economic development. The Iberian section explores towns in both Andalusia and Alentejo, cross border regions in the southwest of Spain and the south of Portugal. Blanca Del Espino Hidalgo in "Miraculous Equilibrium. Keys for a Sustainable Network of Small South Iberian Cities," analyses the strategies adopted by town officials from the perspective of the local network of border regions. Finally, the architectural and urbanistic approach to small towns, from a historical point of view, is introduced by the Czech art historian, Martin Horáček: "'The Architectural Rhythm of a Small Town ... Is Very Familiar to Us.' A Small Town as an Aesthetic Ideal of the Twentieth Century."

The aim of the book's authors was to create a multi-faceted collection of studies that would portray different aspects of the contemporary situation of small towns. By means of selected case studies, the notion of the small town is thematized, and its various meanings in different social and geographical settings are assessed. In their research the authors focus on an analysis of the identity of urban communities. This is their first collaboration and followed from the EAUH session proposal on small towns. Their belief that an understanding of small town perspective would make a considerable contribution to the ongoing debate in their respective regions convinced them of the need to research a topic which does not seem so very important, at least at first sight.

The only previous project on European small towns was carried out by Bernard Lepetit and Peter Clark more than 20 years ago, and focussed on the early modern period. There was no further attempt to systematically research small towns in the 19th century and later, on a supranational scale. This is surprising since in Europe small towns remain a quite visible type of urban settlement even in the 21st century, regardless of previous urban growth, regional urbanisation, and the dominant position of metropolises, metropolitan agglomerations, and large cities in general.

Our perspective is of course European, claiming as we do that the number of small towns is still quite large, and that the experience of life and sociability in such a community is important. This is one of the neglected themes in the urban history of the modern and contemporary period, and the gap cannot be filled by one research project or by one book. The notion of the small town in the context of the changes that have occurred in the second half of the 20th century and the beginning of the third millennium deserves to be revisited, and perhaps this study might stimulate the interest of other scholars in the topic.

All the chapters in the book underwent the process of anonymous peer review and critical comments were highly appreciated and integrated by the authors. We would like to express the gratitude of the authors to our colleagues PhDr. Kathleen Brenda Geaney for the linguistic review and Mgr. Iva Sokolová for the careful preparation of the manuscript for printing. Their role was essential in the final stage. Co-authoring the book was a learning process as well as a very agreeable and rewarding experience.

Small Towns as a European Cultural Heritage. Introduction

Luďa Klusáková
and Marie-Vic Ozouf-Marignier

Towns and cities are carriers of the culture of European countries and nations. Alongside iconic metropolises, small towns and their hinterlands are the prevailing type of environment in which people in Europe live. The statistics are very straightforward. Europe is predominantly urban, but, in terms of area, also has 35.1% of intermediate status, and 22.42% mainly rural regions.[1] The map on the site referred to, which shows the distribution of cities according to size, confirms the image of societies where small town experience shapes the lives of a very significant proportion of the population.[2]

Yet these figures notwithstanding, the amount of research that has been devoted to small towns from a comparative European perspective in any period of history is rare. There is of course some but considering how large a proportion of the European population, let alone the global, still live in small towns, it is clear that this topic has suffered neglect among urban historians.[3]

The subject is not new. In France, where the intermediate and primarily rural regions constitute almost sixty five percent (64.95%) of the land area while 77% percent of the population live in cities, we can trace the ups and downs of the association dedicated to the history of small towns, which was very active in the last third of the 20th century, and initiated a series of conferences and collective volumes. This was the period of the decentralization policy introduced by the socialist government of François Mittérand. Nor was interest in the issue confined to France.

---

1 http://ec.europa.eu/eurostat/cache/RSI/#?vis=typologies.urb_typology&lang=en (accessed 16. 9. 2016).

2 http://ec.europa.eu/eurostat/cache/RSI/#?vis=city.statistics&lang=en (accessed 16. 9. 2016).

3 Eveline S. van Leeuwen, *Urban-Rural Interactions. Towns as Focus Points in Rural Development, Contributions to Economics* (Berlin – Heidelberg 2010), 1.

In 1984 the European Council for the Village and Small Town was set up. This campaigning organisation based in the UK has a number of national sections. Although the dynamic behind this body is not at all clear, it confirms the importance of both.[4] It is not surprising either that the German unit of ECOVAST is quite active. Small towns in a peripheral position in Germany represent a very striking phenomenon, as we read in the reports produced by the researchers of *Leibniz-Institut für Regionalentwicklung und Strukturplanung e.V.* (IRS). Of the 1,300 such towns, 75% are characterised by a decline in demographic, economic, and social criteria. This does not mean, of course, that small towns inevitably have to be thus, provided they are prepared to benefit from the regional, cultural landscape and the heritage of small, historic, market towns.[5] This viewpoint is reminiscent of the research carried out by Bernard Kayser on creative urban people in villages and small towns and his typology of the various strategies of *Renaissances Rurales*. His contention is that the fate of small towns, is to a large extent the result of the strategies adopted by those responsible for their governance.[6]

Looking again at France, we find that the last fifteen years has not seen any significant project or publication in the field, despite the fact that France is famous for its regional diversity, which in turn is based on small towns in rural regions and suburban belts surrounding metropolises. In the Czech Republic the ratio between large and small, rural and urban is comparable with France, which is somewhat surprising, but the gap in research on small towns has to be acknowledged. Urban sociology and geography have a slightly larger output. In the early 1990s, Peter Clark, who coordinated a project on small towns in early modern Europe, acknowledged this situation in the editorial preface to the collection of chapters offered for comparative analysis.[7] Twenty years on, the authors of the present study attempted to learn what changes have occurred and, in due course, considered publishing their findings on the grounds that small towns in contemporary Europe are numerous,

---

4   http://www.ecovast.org/english/index%20.htm (accessed 28. 10. 2016).

5   Manfred Kühn, "Small towns in rural areas – What are the possibilities in the periphery? Peripheral Small Towns," IRS Aktuell, *Newsletter for Social Science-Based Spatial Research*, no. 6 (September 2014), 3–4.

6   Bernard Kayser, *La renaissance rurale. Sociologie des campagnes du monde occidental*, (Paris: Armand Colin 1990); Idem, "Les citadins au village," *Espace, populations, sociétés*, *Repopulation et mobilités rurales* (1 February 2001), 152–153. www.persee.fr/doc/espos_0755-7809_2001_num_19_1_1983 (accessed 14. 4. 2017).

7   Peter Clark (ed.), *Small Towns in Early Modern Europe* (Cambridge: Cambridge University Press 1995), xvii.

attractive, difficult in many ways for their inhabitants, and fascinating for the authors of this book. In addition, the problems small towns and their dwellers face are still neglected in historical research.

Over the last decades, rural geography and history have paid attention to the revival of small towns with regard to peri-urbanization and the fight against the desertification of the countryside. The towns themselves have recorded a renewal of interest from people attracted by the quality of the living environment, while the authorities have tried to maintain the services and facilities available at a good level. Heritage and tourism, especially cultural tourism, are becoming important resources for local development. In most European countries, decentralization revalued the role of small towns and gave them more skills and powers. Since the 1990s, European regional policy has demonstrated the importance of social and territorial cohesion. Spatial proximity is seen as a crucial lever for implementing the ideal of solidarity and for generating concerted action in respect of economic growth. Local values, the uniqueness and specificity of a territory or the goods on offer have become successful tools of appeal and competition. National and European public policy, for example the "Leader" program,[8] encourage structuring action in small towns.

The valorisation of "smalltownness" does not come only from the political powers that be. Activism also grows within academic and militant groups. One such is the Society of Territorialists whose leader is the urbanist, Alberto Magnaghi, a professor at the University of Florence. In 2011, the so-called "Territorialist school" began to advocate regional planning based on "urban villages" and local projects. The movement has found a lot of support among local authorities. Though originating in Italy, this network of territorialists has now spread to France. Other initiatives are linked with the creation of defence associations. Since 1990, the Association of small towns of France (APVF) has federated cities from 3,000 to 20,000 inhabitants to promote their specific role in regional and urban planning. It has 1,100 members and is lobbying actively in Parliament and in European institutions. The president of the APVF, Martin Malvy, is also president of the Confederation of Small Towns and Municipalities of the European Union (CTME), which was officially launched in Brussels in 2011. According to its founders, "its aim is to ensure that the voices of Europe's small and medium-sized towns are heard at Euro-

---

8   As a local development approach, and its upgrade – strategy of Community-Led Local Development (CLLD).

pean level and that their interests are fully represented." Mention should also be made of associations whose purpose is to defend small historic towns: the Association of Small Historic Towns and Villages of the UK (ASHTAV) is "an organisation that works to unite amenity and civic societies, parish and town councils in small historic towns and villages throughout Britain." Like several similar institutions in Europe, *I Borghi più belli d'Italia*, founded in March 2001, is an association of small Italian towns of historical interest. This flowering of institutional and militant organisations demonstrates the consciousness of small town identity.

It is not surprising that this movement has resulted in the creation of a European Association of Historic Towns and Regions, which unites the municipal endeavours of a large number of historical towns, many of them small, although size in itself is not an issue.[9] Among its members are individual towns and national associations. It might be expected that in the countries of Central Europe, which has always been classified as a region of small historical urban settlements, these associations would be particularly strong and active. This, however, does not seem to be the case. In the Czech Republic, such an association was founded in 1990 as an NGO.[10] Having as its main goal the preservation, protection and the practical utilization of regional heritage, it had 214 members by 1 August 2016. All of its many diverse activities both for professionals and the public at large are carried out in the Czech Republic and abroad to achieve this objective. Most important among them is the systematic regeneration of urban heritage sites and settlements. Since 1994, the success of this urban regeneration program has been evaluated annually and the "Historical Town of the Year" selected. The association has joined the European Heritage Days – EHD – under the auspices of the Council of Europe and national governmental institutions.

The question as to how the small and historical towns cooperate requires a closer look at the past. The Association of Polish Towns[11] and the Association of Towns and Cities in Slovakia[12] are recently founded bodies. The Association of Towns and Communities of the Czech Repub-

---

9 Heritage Europe was formed as "The European Association of Historic Towns and Regions" by the Council of Europe in October 1999 as part of the initiative "Europe – A Common Heritage." http://www.historic-towns.org/ (accessed 26. 10. 2016).

10 *Sdružení historických sídel Čech, Moravy a Slezska (SHS ČMS)*, http://www.historickasidla.cz/ (accessed 26. 10. 2016).

11 *Związek Miast Polskich*, http://www.zmp.poznan.pl/strona-22-historia.html (accessed 26. 10. 2016).

12 *Združenie miest a obcí Slovenska*, http://www.zmos.sk/ (accessed 26. 10. 2016).

lic,[13] which is a source of important information about the networking of cities, has today more than 2,600 members.[14] The association went through several stages as a result of political conditions.

The association commissioned an article on its origins in which we learn that it all began in 1907 in the historic town of Kolín. There, 210 delegates met and decided to create a formal corporation, as was the case with other estates and professions in the country.[15] In reality, efforts to establish an association of towns had even deeper roots and can be traced to a meeting of city representatives in 1895 – on both occasions, incidentally, the mayors of the cities legitimized their meeting by arguments about the danger of self-government while, at the same time, urging the need to join in efforts to overcome pressure from the government in Vienna. 200 delegates from about one hundred cities met at the 1907 convention. They decided to hold regular meetings and to build an association which would carry out the policies agreed. The main interest of the association was on the governance and functioning of the cities and on regulating their infrastructure. Shortly afterwards, in 1909, the association started a newsletter (Věstník), which illustrates the scope of its activities and interests. While the primary goal was to derive some sort of benefit from unified action, the secondary appears to have been to satisfy curiosity about a parallel situation in the outside world. They studied the experiences of other countries and sought relevant literature on the topic. However, national conditions, tensions between Czech and German cities, and the position of one or other minority within the towns or magistracies themselves preoccupied them. During the Great War, the cities remained faithful to the Austro-Hungarian Empire and the association issued declarations of loyalty to the Hapsburgs in Vienna. In 1918, interestingly, the main topic for debate was the supply of alimentary products to the cities.

After the establishment of the independent state, the cities could continue to function as an organised body, since they had never ceased in this activity. In fact, they claimed that it was the cities which were building the new state and were the major investor in the infrastructure. City finances, however, were in a difficult state after the war. In 1920, the association met for the first time in the new state and invited representa-

---

13 *Svaz měst a obcí České republiky* (SMO ČR).

14 http://www.smocr.cz/cz/svaz-mest-a-obci-cr/kdo-jsme/kdo-jsme.aspx (accessed 26. 10. 2016).

15 Lenka Zgrajová, *Svaz měst a obcí očima století* [Cities and Communities Association in Historical Perspective], 2009, http://smocr.cz/o-svazu/z-historie/koreny-svazu.aspx (accessed 14. 4. 2017).

tives from all the 155 national cities to attend, regardless of whether or not they were members of the association.

After World War II, the political authorities viewed the association as a rival and this led to its termination. 1960 witnessed a revival but closure again followed with the defeat of the reforms introduced in 1968. The association re-opened in the last decade of the 20th century, when it became an important partner in the efforts to develop regional politics and networking between the regions and the EU. The Czech association is also a member of the international European body: The Council of European Municipalities and Regions (CEMR).[16]

This association was founded in Geneva in 1951 by a group of European mayors. Later, it expanded to include the regions and become what it is today – the largest organisation for local and regional government in Europe. Its membership comprises more than 50 national associations of towns, municipalities and regions from 40 countries. Together these associations represent some 100,000 local and regional authorities.

The second such association, United Cities and Local Governments (UCLG), represents and defends the interests of local governments on the world stage, regardless of the size of the communities they serve. Headquartered in Barcelona, the organisation's stated mission is: "To be the united voice and world advocate of democratic local self-government, promoting its values, objectives and interests, through cooperation between local governments, and within the wider international community." A targeted work program has been developed which focuses on:

- Increasing the role and influence of local government and its representative organisations in global governance;
- Becoming the main source of support for democratic, effective, innovative local government close to the citizen;
- Ensuring an effective and democratic global organisation. United Cities and Local Governments supports international cooperation between cities and their associations, and facilitates programs, networks and partnerships to build the capacity of local governments. It promotes the role of women in local decision-making, and is a gateway to relevant information on local government across the world.[17]

The association is organised into workgroups, in which cities and local governments from all continents are represented, although Europe is

16 The Council of European Municipalities and Regions http://www.ccre.org/en (accessed 4. 4. 2017).
17 United Cities and Local Governments (UCLG), http://www.cities-localgovernments.org/sections.asp (accessed 3. 3. 2012).

somewhat underrepresented. Very active are the French representatives, who are numerous. Central Europe was represented on about eight occasions by German delegates, twice by Slovak, and twice by Polish, but not by Czechs or Hungarians or indeed any other nationality which declares itself Central European.

When we delve more into the past, we find other associations with the specific goal of promoting cultural heritage, such as those affiliated with UNESCO and associations promoting the culture of peace. In Spanish Guernica in 1987, the 50th anniversary of the bombing was commemorated. The town hosted the Preliminary Congress of the World Union of Cities for Peace. The full congress was subsequently held in Madrid, bringing together representatives of cities from all over the world. Since then, Guernica-Lumo has been a member of this association.[18] While information on its activities is somewhat lacking in cyber space, it does point to another association which promotes the culture of peace: the International Association of Peace Messenger Cities[19]. This was founded in 1987, and among its founding members were several central European capital cities, including Prague, Vienna and Warsaw.

The impetus behind this association is likewise rooted in the past, to the years shortly after the end of World War II, when the many destroyed cities in Europe (Warsaw, Oswiencim-Auschwitz, Volgograd, Saint Petersburg), as well as Asia (Hiroshima and Nagasaki in Japan) evoked sympathy and support for recovery. The International Cities of Peace[20] organisation stems from the idea of town-twinning. The aim is to create occasions for citizens of European cities to come together, learn about one another, and thus help to overcome prejudices and prevent another military conflict in Europe.

Since Central European cities are often missing from global networks, other ways of enhancing cooperation among them, such as individual contacts, or regional and micro-regional networks, have to be explored. It is not clear why their contribution is overlooked. Is it a question of self-centred interests at play or perhaps a lack of funding to cover membership costs? The Partnership/Twinning movement, creating as

---

18 http://www.gernika-lumo.net/datu_orokorrak/in_historia.htm (accessed 3. 3. 2012); World Union of Cities for Peace (WUCP) http://www.uia.org/s/or/en/1100046107 (accessed 4. 4. 2017).

19 International Association of Peace Messenger Cities, http://www.iapmc.org/cities.aspx (accessed 3. 3. 2012).

20 The International Cities of Peace Organization, http://www.internationalcitiesofpeace.org /what/what.html (accessed 3. 3. 2012).

it does opportunities for real meeting of citizens, personal interaction and friendship, is viewed as an effective tool to support cohesion and effectively help EU integration.[21]

The association identifies three types of interaction. (1) On the local scale, micro-regional, and regional: today very much linked to EU projects and EU funding, this band encompasses those peripheral European regions which cross state boundaries and always revolve around centres on either side of borders. Inclusion/exclusion is categorized on a territorial basis. However, although the network is similarly defined, it does not respect state territorial borders. (2) On the national / state scale: this comprises national networks of cities and is highly inclusive with members obliged to accept the constitution of the association. (3) On the international level: here larger networks cover macro-regions. Membership is voluntary and motivation has to come from within the city's leadership. The three levels of collaboration however have different goals. The first is to overcome peripherality and local difficulties, the second to surmount problems of urban financing and governance, and limitations to self-government. The third level points to macro-regional interests and global issues. The associations however do not help to resolve our primary question about the link between size and function.

What is a town and when is a town considered to be a small town? What does small town actually mean? Urban history research provides no clear-cut answers to these two questions. Although functional definitions are applied in urban studies, a comparative overview of the situation in a number of European countries displays a large variety of approaches.[22] Vincent Houillon and Laurence Thomsin discovered that even at the beginning of the third millennium some towns and cities are defined by their status in state administration, while demographic criteria are used in others. With this in mind, we have left the authors free to formulate their own definition of a small town as befitting their own particular study. From the perspective of the English countryside, it is a town with fewer than 10,000 inhabitants. From the Spanish perspective, we are faced with a set of towns functioning in a network, representing

---

21 Svaz měst a obcí České republiky [The Association of Cities and Communities of Czech Republic] http://smocr.cz/ (accessed 4. 4. 2017); http://smocr.cz/cz/partnerstvi-mest/default.aspx (accessed 3. 3. 2012, this page does not exist anymore, returning visitor to http://smocr.cz/ and consequently to http://www.partnerskamesta.cz/ (accessed 15. 4. 2017).

22 Vincent Houillon – Laurence Thomsin, "Définitions du rural et de l'urbain dans quelques pays européens," *Espace, populations, sociétés*, 2001-1-2, Repopulation et mobilités rurales, 195–200. http://www.persee.fr/web/revues/home/prescript/article/espos_0755-7809_2001 _num_19_1_1989 (accessed 4. 4. 2017).

60% of the land structure, of indeterminate dimension, but which far from decaying are actually growing in size and population. The chapter on Greece, on the other hand, looks at the overwhelming position of the capital city compared to that of small towns, a subject few historians are interested in and about which we know little. What a small town is in the Greek context we learn from the example of Rethymno, a central town on the island of Crete, which, despite its regional function, is thus classified. A different slant on "smalltownness" emerges from the chapter on the provincial Russian town of Myshkin. The authors follow the perspective of small towns in contrast with metropolises as formulated by Georg Simmel. A small town is above all a local community bound by cohesion and solidarity which help it survive. Primary relationships and a focus on collectivity are what define a small town.[23]

The threshold of urbanity and "smalltownness" thus cannot be definitively set for all the case studies presented. From the outset, the aim has not been to produce a complex, systematic survey. To the contrary, the book has been conceived as an exploration, a probe into the research area.

As mentioned in the Preface, the idea of the book emerged from a session at the international conference held by the European Association of Urban History in Lisbon in 2014. Its purpose was to revisit, from an interdisciplinary perspective, the notion of small towns in the context of the changes that occurred in the second half of the 20th century. Our call had a very good response with over twenty proposals received from urban geographers, architects, anthropologists, and historians, thereby confirming our belief that we had chosen an important issue.

Contributions were sought which would address a set of questions:

- What is understood by small town in academic and public discourse and in other areas?
- Are small towns defined primarily by population size, by their social functions, or by other criteria, such as morphology or distinctive culture?
- Have small towns simply been shrinking, losing population, and even dying since the 19th century, or have they shown a capacity for sustainability and growth as well?
- Are their economic, cultural and social functions disappearing? Do they still retain administrative functions?

---

23   Greg Yudin and Yulia Koloshenko quote Georg Simmel, "The metropolis and mental life," in *The Blackwell City Reader*, edited by Gary Bridge and Sophie Watson (Chichester 2010), 107.

- How has globalisation influenced the fortunes of small towns?
- What strategies have been adopted by local and regional officials to keep small towns alive, to cope with the small town condition, and to overcome the stigma of "smalltownness?"
- What frames of identification are used in the (self) presentation of small towns? Do they relate to local, regional, national, or supranational contexts?
- Is history important for small towns? How are history and memory used for the representation and socialisation of their society? How do small towns react to musealization?
- How do small towns perceive and portray their position with regard to the border between urban and rural? With which side do they identify? Do they play with their "urban" nature and "urban" past?

The session generated a small group of authors who wished to continue the debate and offered the five chapters which make up this volume. They have in common a concern for historical and cultural heritage, for what small towns understand as heritage and how it is treated by them. Geographically, the scope of the work stretches across Europe, touching towns in England, Spain, Portugal, Greece, the Czech and Moravian lands, and Russia. In all five case studies the small town as a cultural product, and its place in the European cultural heritage, is discussed. The chapters examine a variety of different towns which the authors, respecting the rules of their national statistical institutes and the research criteria, consider small. Saying that a town is a cultural product implies that we have accepted a constructivist approach and are analysing a process, a continuum, resulting from the efforts of individuals who have been following their own goals and interests.

The first chapter written by Tom Hulme and his colleagues Angela Bartie, Linda Fleming, Mark Freeman, and Paul Readman highlights a traditional amusement organized in small towns in England, historical pageantry, which had its heyday in the first half of the twentieth century and appeared still in the 1950s. Long and rich in presentation of important events, pageants virtually disappeared in the second half of the century. According to the authors, historical shows staged in the second half of the century were shorter, featuring only episodes from history. The authors call the events, which emerged in England in the 1970s and 1980s, a community play, and as such they indeed served. And wherever they appear now, they have a similar purpose although they are not presented as the successor of pageantry. The authors focus on the case of Axbridge, where the shows were staged even in 2000 and 2010 as an argument supporting the thesis about their instrumental use in revitalization strategies. However, the very popular reconstruction of historic events, such as the Battle of Austerlitz or the Royal Coronation of Charles IV in September 2016 in Prague, suggest, that pageantry is by no means a dead tradition nor confined only to the social life of small English towns.

In his chapter, Martin Horáček deals with the theme of small towns from the perspective of architectural historiography. One of the recurring topics in urban planning in the last century was the criticism of over-sized cities combined with proposals for alternative kinds of residential sites. These reports may be a source for clarifying our understanding of "smalltownness." At the turn of the 20th century, several writers support-ed the garden city movement. Others highlighted historical small towns and tried not only to protect their surviving appearance but also to turn them into a model for architects and urban planners. They considered small towns user-friendly, healthy and, indeed, beautiful. Art historians, architects and heritage conservationists began to study the morphology of small towns, their specific street layouts and the relationship between various types of buildings. Based on such studies they formulated de-sign codes for future planning. Belief in the vitality of small towns had been fostered by supporters of the *Heimatschutz* movement in Germany, Austria and Switzerland until World War II, as well as by influential art critics and architects in interwar Czechoslovakia. In the decades of eco-nomic growth after the war, the small-town ideal seemed to disappear; however, new criticism of the "modern ugliness" of cities led to a revival of interest in the aesthetic qualities of small towns. Following a general overview, this study focuses on two important defenders of the charm of traditional small towns in the Czech Lands – Zdeněk Wirth and Jiří Kroha. Wirth, an art historian and heritage conservator, persuaded archi-tects to imitate the small town architectural patterns which existed before the Great War. On the other hand, Kroha, an architect and influential communist ideologue, juxtaposed the design of small towns against the reinforced concrete high-rise housing estates of the 1960s. Using the arguments presented by Wirth and Kroha, the study compares and contrasts the promotion of the small town ideal in the capitalist period and the postwar communist era.

The Spanish/Portuguese case study written by the architect Blanca del Espino shows how provincial rural towns are interacting with smaller settlements nearby. Coping with the decline of their agricultural function on the one hand and adapting to a new role, be it industrial, tourist, or services, on the other, these towns are undergoing a process of transformation. Two urban networks – one in the Spanish province of Andalusia, the other in Portuguese Alentejo – are used to illustrate cross border regional transactions. The two towns of Lucena in Andalusia and Beja in Alentejo point up contrasts and tensions between economic and urban interests. Del Espino also discusses the role of heritage in the process of small town adaptation as a success story from the southern part of the Iberian Peninsula.

The Greek chapter, the case study of Rethymno, was also written by an architect. Olga Moatsou is concerned with one town on the island of Crete, a case of *pars pro toto*, viewing the island's small town capital Rethymno in the context of the national urban network. An amalgam of historical layers suggesting overlapping identities typical of small towns on the Greek islands as well as on mainland Greece itself, Rethymno stagnated until the 1960s when tourism paved the way to new economic conditions and growth. For these towns, historicity and the way it is used are the author's main concern.

Greg Yudin and Yulia Koloshenko discuss the multiple modes of historical work that contribute to the development of tourism in small towns in a close analysis of the case of Myshkin. This town has achieved tourist glory through the construction of a myth, a false story strictly speaking. Tourism is an especially attractive economic solution for many small towns facing the challenges of the global economy. However, building an efficient tourist industry requires learning how to manufacture specific tourist experiences. Sometimes, the creation of an appealing myth can make a town more attractive to visitors than a careful reconstruction of its history. Yet it might well be asked if this kind of constructivist approach facilitates the creation of a sustainable community capable of maintaining the tourist experience. The study shows that building a proactive local community demands both preserving and inventing local history and tradition. By analysing the successful development of tourism in a small Russian town, the authors explain how constructing phantasy and safeguarding authenticity reinforce each other and provide a variety of opportunities for tourism and the indigenous inhabitants.

Thus the five chapters display five cases of small towns which were products of national and regional cultures, and represented varieties of "smalltownness." They have a common interest in the valorisation of heritage, culture based on historicity, which is rediscovered, rehabilitated, reconstructed, and in one case constructed, as an emerging heritage. History is shown to have a double function: it is a tool to enable a town's adaptation to new circumstances and, simultaneously, it facilitates the construction of a town's unique identity. History, its interpretation and management, plays an undeniable part in the production of a small town's culture. How history is interpreted and used stems from cultural traditions. The authors are convinced that through the variety of approaches and cases presented they can contribute to a better understanding of the role of small towns in European urban development.

Performing the Past: Identity, Civic Culture and Historical Pageants in Twentieth-Century English Small Towns

Angela Bartie, Linda Fleming, Mark Freeman, Tom Hulme and Paul Readman[1]

Stephen Royle, in *The Cambridge Urban History of Britain* (2000), defined a small town, in the period 1850–1950, as a place with fewer than 10,000 people, but with a greater "variety of functions" than villages.[2] More recently, in 2011, the association Small Towns for Tomorrow used a larger definition of urban areas with under 40,000 inhabitants.[3] Regardless of the definition used, historians have mostly been in agreement in seeing the economic and cultural position of the small town in twentieth-century Britain as a precarious one – though it should be noted that this consensus has been reached despite the relative lack of work on small towns themselves, which have proved less popular than cities as subjects of study.[4] As Britain urbanised from the mid-nineteenth century, and industrialised cities grew rapidly, the number of small towns in Britain, as defined by Royle, fell, from 923 in 1851 to 748 in 1951.[5] Even using

---

1 The research on which this chapter is based was funded by the Arts and Humanities Research Council, award number AH/K003887/1. For further details of the project, see http://www. historicalpageants.ac.uk/.

2 Stephen A. Royle, "The development of small towns in Britain," in *Cambridge Urban History of Britain, Volume III*, edited by Martin Daunton (Cambridge: Cambridge University Press 2000), 152; Robert E. Dickinson, "The distribution and functions of the smaller urban settlements of East Anglia," *Geography* 17 (1932), 20.

3 Alison Eardley, ed., *Small Towns of the Future, Not the Past*, (September 2011), 5. http://www. smalltownsfortomorrow.org/wp-content/uploads/2011/07/STfT-Essay1-WEB.pdf (accessed 19. 4. 2017).

4 As one historian has recently remarked, "The small country town in modern England has attracted very little specific historical consideration." Arthur Burns, "Beyond the 'Red Vicar': Community and christian socialism in Thaxted, Essex, 1910–1984," *History Workshop Journal* 75 (2013), 107.

5 Royle, "Development of small towns," 153.

the larger definition, comprising towns with fewer than 40,000 people, it is still clear that small towns have gradually lost out in several ways to larger urban areas.[6] A concentration of economic power in regional powerhouse cities and an improved transport network has diminished the role of local capital and market functions in the twentieth-century small-town economy.[7] Such a process was compounded by the economic effect of two world wars and the interwar depression, the effects of which were particularly heavy in smaller places.[8] In administrative terms the post-Second World War era also saw the further ascension of the central state, weakening local systems of government – or, following the Local Government Acts of 1972 and 1974, abolishing them altogether.[9]

It seems naturally to follow that, for the above reasons, local culture also declined. Certainly, this interpretation has predominated. Historians have identified powerful nationalising trends that had wide purchase across Britain from the early twentieth century onwards. Among other things, historians have pointed to the diminishing importance of the provincial press from its late nineteenth-century heyday, and the ebbing away of the local-based philanthropic activity and civic initiatives – various societies, athenaeums, libraries and other charities – that had added so much to the vitality of Victorian urban life.[10] To this might be added an emphasis on the decline in the autonomy of municipal authorities, as state power became increasingly centralised, and with this the replacement of older forms of locally rooted political cultures with a newer electoral politics based on mass national organisations,

---

6   Eardley, ed., *Small Towns of the Future*, 5.
7   Royle, "Development of small towns," 166, 169, 172.
8   Ibid., 179.
9   John P. R. M. Redcliffe-Maud and Bruce Wood, *English Local Government Reformed* (London: Oxford University Press 1974); Jerry White, "From Herbert Morrison to command and control: the decline of local democracy and its effect on public services," *History Workshop Journal* 59 (2005), 76; Gordon Morris, *Small Towns, Big Societies*, Essay No. 2 (November 2011), 1 http://www.smalltownsfortomorrow.org/wp-content/uploads/2011/10/STfT_Essay2_WEB. pdf (accessed 19. 4. 2017); Derek Fraser, *The Evolution of the British Welfare State: A History of Social Policy since the Industrial Revolution,* 4th ed., (Basingstoke 2009), 209–210; John Davis, "Central government and the towns," in *Cambridge Urban History of Britain*, 272.
10   Simon Gunn, *The Public Culture of the Victorian Middle Class* (Manchester: Manchester University Press 2000); Stephen Koss, *The Rise and Fall of the Political Press in Britain, Volume II: The Twentieth Century* (London: Hamish Hamilton 1984). For a useful survey of the scholarship, see Richard H. Trainor, "The 'decline' of British urban governance since 1850: a reassessment." In *Urban Governance: Britain and Beyond since 1750*, ed.Robert J. Morris and Richard H. Trainor (Aldershot: Ashgate 2000), 29–32.

general party programmes, and appeals to class interest.[11] Even large cities have been portrayed as being affected by such nationalising trends, as country and empire assumed cultural dominance, and "Englishness" overpowered localism and provincial identities.[12] Manifestations of national and imperial patriotism grew rapidly, encouraged by nationwide cultural institutions, events, and days of remembrance.[13] While these trends were already evident in the Edwardian era, the First World War clarified and accelerated the process – or so it has been claimed.[14] The Second World War had further socially unifying effects, and a "national" culture was promoted by cultural institutions, most notably the BBC, as well as events such as the Festival of Britain (1951) and the Coronation of Queen Elizabeth II (1953). These developments, it has been argued, undermined localism both politically and culturally.[15]

Recent research on the interwar period in particular, however, has taken a more nuanced approach to the narrative of "decline." A number of political historians have emphasised the persistence of "the politics of place" deep into the twentieth century. As Jon Lawrence and Duncan Tanner have shown, the early advances of the Labour Party were importantly determined by local factors, while other scholars have pointed to

11 See Jon Lawrence and Miles Taylor, "Introduction: electoral sociology and the historians." In *Party, State, and Society: Electoral Behaviour in Britain since 1820*, edited by Jon Lawrence and Miles Taylor (Aldershot: Scolar Press 1997), 1–26.

12 Anne B. Rodrick, *Self-Help and Civic Culture: Citizenship in Victorian Birmingham* (Ashgate 2004) 205–206; Brian Doyle, "The invention of English." In *Englishness: Politics and Culture 1880–1920*, ed. Robert Colls and Philip Dodd (London: Croom Helm 1986).

13 Richard Weight and Abigail Beach, "Introduction." In *The Right to Belong: Citizenship and National Identity in Britain, 1930–1960*, edited by Richard Weight and Abigail Beach (London: I. B. Tauris 1998), 1; Sian Nicholas, "From John Bull to John Citizen: images of national identity and citizenship on the wartime BBC." In Weight and Beach, *The Right to Belong*, 39; Jim English, "Empire Day in Britain, 1904–1958," *Historical Journal* 49 (2006), 247–248; Brad Beaven and John Griffiths, "Creating the exemplary citizen: the changing notion of citizenship in Britain 1870–1939," *Contemporary British History* 22 (2008), 211–212; Julia Stapleton, "Citizenship versus patriotism in twentieth-century England," *Historical Journal* 48 (2005), 164–166.

14 Nicoletta F. Gullace, *"The Blood of Our Sons": Men, Women and the Renegotiation of British Citizenship During the Great War* (Basingstoke: Palgrave Macmillan 2002), 4; Matthew C. Hendley, *Organized Patriotism and the Crucible of War: Popular Imperialism in Britain, 1914–1932* (Montreal: McGill-Queen's University Press 2012), 3; Jay M. Winter, "British national identity and the First World War." In *The Boundaries of the State in Modern Britain*, ed. S. J. D. Green and Richard C. Whiting (Cambridge: Cambridge University Press 2002), 261–277.

15 Thomas Hajkowski, *The BBC and National Identity in Britain 1922–1953*, (Manchester: Manchester University Press 2010). Chandler has also argued that the rise of central government during and after the Second World War led to a loss of local government power: see John A. Chandler, *Explaining Local Government: Local Government in Britain Since 1800* (Manchester: Manchester University Press 2007), 184.

the continued (if declining) importance of the provincial press in shaping electoral outcomes in the 1920s and 1930s.[16] Still more relevant to our purposes here, case studies by urban historians have uncovered vibrant local cultures;[17] shown how local authorities retained autonomy in the delivery of services despite central funding controls;[18] challenged the accusation of municipal lethargy in public health provision;[19] demonstrated how imperial discourse was filtered through the perspective of localities;[20] and questioned the decline of middle-class governance.[21] Although these studies are welcome additions to the continuing interpretation of civic culture, they have mainly concentrated on large industrial cities, and tend to overlook the experience of smaller urban centres.

A significant aspect of this research has been the recognition of the part that public rituals, celebrations and commemorative events could play in the stimulation of local civic culture. One example was the historical pageant, as studies of Leicester and Manchester have noted.[22] Historical pageants are the focus of this chapter. They took the form of a theatrical representation of a series of distinct historical episodes, usually around ten, performed by a cast of hundreds – and sometimes thousands – in an open-air arena. A town's pageant would usually be

16 Duncan Tanner, *Political Change and the Labour Party 1900–1918* (Cambridge: Cambridge University Press 1990); Duncan Tanner, "The Labour Party and electoral politics in the coalfields," in *Miners, Unions, and Politics, 1910–47*, edited by Alan Campbell, Nina Fishman and David Howell (Aldershot: Scolar Press 1996), 59–92; Jon Lawrence, *Speaking for the People: Party, Language and Popular Politics in England, 1867–1914* (Cambridge: Cambridge University Press 1998), 227–240; Michael Dawson, "Party politics and the provincial press in early twentieth-century England," *Twentieth Century British History* 9 (1998), 201–218; Paul Gliddon, "The political importance of provincial newspapers, 1903–1945: The Rowntrees and the Liberal press," *Twentieth Century British History* 14 (2003), 24–42.

17 Charlotte Wildman, "Urban transformation in Liverpool and Manchester, 1918–1939," *Historical Journal* 55 (2012), 119–143; Siobhan Begley, "Voluntary associations and the civic ideal in Leicester, 1870–1939," PhD thesis (University of Leicester 2009).

18 Shane Ewen, "Power and administration in two Midland cities," PhD thesis, (University of Leicester 2003), 246–247; Nick Hayes, "Civic perceptions: Housing and local decision-making in English cities in the 1920s," *Urban History* 27 (2000), 211–233.

19 Martin Gorsky, "Public health in interwar England and Wales: Did it fail?," *Dynamis* 28 (2008), 175–198.

20 Brad Beaven, *Visions of Empire: Patriotism, Popular Culture and the City, 1870–1939*, (Manchester: Manchester University Press 2012), 208.

21 Nick Hayes, "Counting civil society: Deconstruction elite participation in the provincial English city, 1900–1950," *Urban History* 40 (2013), 287–314. See also Trainor, "The 'decline' of British urban governance," 28–46.

22 Tom Hulme, "Civic culture and citizenship: The Nature of urban governance in interwar Manchester and Chicago," PhD thesis (University of Leicester 2013); Begley, "Voluntary associations and the civic ideal."

performed on several successive days, in front of large paying audiences assembled in grandstands constructed specially for the event. Historical pageants were significant in promoting the civic culture of smaller towns, as Mark Freeman's recent work on the St Albans pageants has shown.[23] Located in Hertfordshire, within twenty miles of London, and with a mixed population of industrial workers and commuters, St Albans underwent significant expansion in the first half of the twentieth century, so that by 1939 it no longer fitted even the larger definition of a small town: the population had reached 42,450.[24] It had two large postwar historical pageants, in 1948 and 1953, which demonstrated the ongoing cultural resonance of localism even in a period that saw political and administrative centralisation, as well as planned urban expansion that seemed to jeopardise the sense of identity in towns like St Albans.

In this chapter we focus on urban centres that were even smaller than St Albans, offering a general assessment of historical pageantry in a range of small towns. In doing so, we deepen and amplify the critique of the idea that local culture and civic feeling have necessarily declined from the Edwardian period onwards, showing that this critique has traction in relation to the experiences of small as well as large urban centres. We consider both the social organisation of pageants and the themes they portrayed, and present two main lines of argument: first, that historical pageants could create local feelings of a shared past and future, while making a claim of importance for a small town in a wider national history; and second, that these performances could also effectively vitalise civic culture in the pursuit of a common goal. While we acknowledge the specific difficulties that both the pageantry movement and small towns faced in the post-Second World War era, we will present a case study of the small Somerset town of Axbridge to demonstrate that decline was never predetermined. For the purposes of this chapter we will concentrate on towns with populations (at the time of their pageants) smaller than 25,000 – half-way between the definitions supplied by Royle (10,000) and Small Towns for Tomorrow (40,000). While this set of parameters is perhaps crude, it allows for a comparative focus upon towns that grew during the century, while still retaining many of the cultural features associated with small towns even as their population exceeded 10,000.

23　Mark Freeman, "'Splendid display, *pompous* spectacle': historical pageants in twentieth-century Britain," *Social History* 38 (2013), 423–455.

24　Mark Freeman, *St Albans: A History*, (Lancaster: Carnegie Publishing 2008), 257. St Albans had become a city in 1877, but at that time its population was only around 10,000.

Although we focus here on the experience of small English towns, it should be noted that historical pageants also featured prominently in the cultures of other British nations, and in many other countries, too. Many small towns in Scotland had pageants during the twentieth century; indeed, from 1947 to 2005, no fewer than eighteen were staged at the ruined abbey in Arbroath (population 24,000).[25] As Joan Fitz Patrick Dean's recent work has shown, pageants were also a significant cultural phenomenon in Ireland.[26] In Germany, pageants formed one element of the larger twentieth-century *Heimat* movement, which celebrated particular localities' contributions to the wider story of German nationhood.[27] *Heimat* was important even in divided post-war Germany: for example, historical pageants – processional, rather than episodic, in form – were a common feature of many anniversary festivals in the small towns of the German Democratic Republic.[28] Perhaps most notably, the pageant craze took strong hold in the United States, in the vanguard of modernity, achieving particular significance in small towns, as David Glassberg has shown.[29]

1. Small-town patriotism

The twentieth-century historical pageant movement can be traced to the small town of Sherborne, in Dorset, which put on an enormously successful pageant in 1905. Staged in the ruins of Sherborne Castle, its style, organisation and themes were consistently replicated when "pageant fever" or "pageantitis" consequently swept the nation. The Sherborne pageant was the brainchild of Louis Napoleon Parker, a French-born English/American composer and playwright who had previously worked at Sherborne School between 1877 and 1892 (see Figure 1). Drawing on a wide range influences – such as the passion play of Oberammergau,

---

25 Linda Fleming, "'Not for Glory, Nor for Wealth ... For Freedom!' The Arbroath Abbey Pageant, 1949 ... and a few others," http://www.historicalpageants.ac.uk/featured-pageants/arbroath-abbey-pageant-1949/ (accessed 15. 11. 2015).

26 Joan FitzPatrick Dean, *All Dressed Up: Modern Irish Historical Pageantry* (Syracuse, NY: Syracuse University Press 2014).

27 Jan Palmowski, *Inventing a Socialist Nation: Heimat and the Politics of Everyday Life in the GDR, 1945–1990* (Cambridge: Cambridge University Press 2009); Celia Applegate, *A Nation of Provincials: The German Idea of Heimat* (Berkeley: University of California Press 1990); Elizabeth Boa and Rachel Palfreyman, *Heimat: A German Dream*, (Oxford: Oxford University Press 2000).

28 Palmowski, *Inventing a Socialist Nation*, 138–146.

29 David Glassberg, *American Historical Pageantry*, (Chapel Hill, NC: University of North Carolina Press 1990).

L.N.P. inventing it

Fig. 1: Louis Napoleon Parker "inventing" the historical pageant. Source: Postcard in the authors' possession.

the resurgence of Morris dancing, Wagnerian theatre and Shakespeare – Parker established the basic theatrical format of historical pageantry, one which was very largely adhered to across the twentieth century.[30] In June 1904, well before the actual production of the Sherborne pageant, Parker had already stipulated that "certain broad lines" were necessary: an entire absence of the professional element; all actors, singers, and instrumentalists to be drawn from the locality; each performer to pay for or make their own costume; and large provision for absolutely free admission.[31] In the wake of his success at Sherborne, Parker put on a string of pageants in other places, including Warwick, Dover, Colchester and Bury St Edmunds.

---

30 Ayako Yoshino, *Pageant Fever: Local History and Consumerism in Edwardian England* (Tokyo: Waseda University Press 2011); Deborah Sugg Ryan, "'Pageantitis': Frank Lascelles' 1907 Oxford historical pageant, visual spectacle and popular memory," *Visual Culture in Britain* 8 (2007), 63–82; Cecil P. Goodden, *The Story of the Sherborne Pageant* (Sherborne: no publisher named 1906), 11; "Historic pageant at Sherborne," *Review of Reviews*, June 1905, 631; Roy Judge, "Merrie England and the Morris 1881–1910," *Folklore* 104 (1993), 135; Michael Dobson, *Shakespeare and Amateur Performance: A Cultural History*, (Cambridge: Cambridge University Press 2011), 168–169.

31 Goodden, *Story of the Sherborne Pageant*, 11.

Historical pageantry spread rapidly in the Edwardian period. Although its strength ebbed and flowed, the movement remained an important feature of British cultural life across much of the twentieth century; cumulatively, there have been many hundreds of large-scale historical pageants, as well as countless village-, church- and school-organised performances.[32] Yet despite the significance of the phenomenon, it is only relatively recently that scholars have begun to pay sustained attention to the movement. They have done so from a variety of perspectives, exploring pageants in relation to literary and historical culture, social history, and biography.[33] The launch in 2013 of the major Arts and Humanities Research Council-funded "Redress of the Past" project has given further impetus to research in the area, but, as of yet, the particular place of small towns has not been analysed.[34]

But, from the beginning, the historical pageant format was particularly apt for small towns. Sherborne, with 6,000 inhabitants, was apparently bypassed by tourists heading for the coasts of Cornwall and Devon; realising the potential of its small size was thus fundamental to the projected narrative of the event.[35] Indeed, the promotional material of the pageant drew attention to the impression that the town had previously "seemed to be almost sinking into old age and decay" – as did Parker, too, in the initial organisational meetings.[36] This perspective also made its way into the press; in June 1905 the *Daily Express,* for example, described how "A year ago Sherborne [...] was perhaps a dull enough place to live in [...]. But from its slumbering-place a magic wand has called forth Sherborne's soul, and the little town throbs with a new and quicker life."[37] According to Parker, in an interview with the *Daily Mail,* it was the publication of W. B. Wildman's *A Short History of Sherborne* in

---

32 Ryan estimates, conservatively, that there were at least forty before 1914: Ryan, "'Pageantitis,'" 64.

33 See, for example, Michael Woods, "Performing power: local politics and the Taunton pageant of 1928," *Journal of Historical Geography* 25 (1999), 57–74; Ayako Yoshino, "'Between the acts' and Louis Napoleon Parker – the creator of the modern English pageant," *Critical Survey* 15, no. 2 (2003), 49–60; Paul Readman, "The place of the past in English culture c. 1890–1914," *Past and Present* 186 (2005), 147–199; Jed Esty, *A Shrinking Island: Modernism and National Culture in England* (Princeton, NJ: Princeton University Press 2004), esp. 54ff.

34 See http://www.historicalpageants.ac.uk/ (accessed 19. 4. 2017).

35 Chalmers Roberts, "The Sherborne Pageant," *The World's Work and Play* 6 (June 1905); *The Sherborne Pageant: Full Report of the Preliminary Meeting, held in the Digby Assembly Rooms, on Thursday, July 14th, 1904* (Sherborne 1904). Dorset History Centre: PE/SH: PA1/1.

36 *Sherborne Pageant: An Unique Historical Spectacle or Folk Play* (Sherborne 1905), 1–2. Dorset History Centre: PE/SH: PA2/3-2/4.

37 "The Sherborne pageant," *Daily Express* (20 June 1905), 4.

1896, with a second edition in 1902, that first "led to a revival of inter-est" in the town; Parker capitalised on this reassertion of place to bring Sherborne to the front of national consciousness with the first historical pageant of the modern era.[38] Over 30,000 people saw the pageant, and it made an impressive profit of £1,872, as well as providing a valuable boost to local businesses.[39]

Other small towns were quick to recognise Sherborne's success and the potential profit and publicity a pageant could bring. Romsey, with a population of around 4,000, celebrated its millenary in 1907 with four successful performances of a ten-episode pageant, each seen by between 3,000 and 4,000 people, and made a healthy profit of £548.[40] Before the First World War at least ten small towns staged similar pageants. These included St Albans in 1907 (population c. 17,500), Hertford in 1914 (population c. 7,500), Stafford in 1913 (population c. 20,000), Thirsk in 1907 (population c. 12,000) and Bury St Edmunds in 1907 (population c. 16,000).[41] And while such small-town pageants were not always success-ful in purely financial terms, as measured for instance by ticket income or souvenir sales, contemporaries were quick to laud the exposure the town had received. For the duration of a pageant, the place became the "hero," and it was common for the whole town to be a part of the celebration, decorated profusely with bunting, flowers, and advertising.[42]

If historical pageants were geared towards bringing crowds of visi-tors to the small town, advertising its products and services as well as making a small profit, there were also more lofty ideals at play. From the beginning of the movement Louis Napoleon Parker had emphasised the effect pageantry could have in awakening local civic pride, arguing that local and national patriotism were constitutive of each other, since "out of local patriotism, I think, springs a far finer national patriotism than any founded merely on rifle-clubs and Morris tubes."[43] The Times, too,

---

38 "St. Aldhelm Celebration: The 'Daily Mail's interview with Mr. Louis Parker." Dorset history centre: PE/SH: PA3/1 – newspaper cutting, presumably from the Daily Mail; William B. Wild-man, A Short History of Sherborne from 705 AD (Sherborne: F. Bennett 1896). Wildman was a teacher at Sherborne School. His book proved successful, a third edition was published in 1911.

39 "The Sherborne pageant," Taunton Courier and Western Advertiser (21 June 1905), 2.

40 Hampshire Chronicle and General Advertiser (29 June 1907), 10–11.

41 All figures taken from census records at Vision of Britain. http://www.visionofbritain.org.uk/ (accessed 19. 4. 2017).

42 Mark Freeman, "Splendid display; pompous spectacle," 442; "The Sherborne pageant," The Times (13 June 1905), 4.

43 Louis N. Parker, "Historical pageants," Journal of the Society of Arts (22 December 1905), 142. Inserted in the barrel of an ordinary service rifle, a Morris tube allowed smaller calibre rounds to be used in drill hall training, so avoiding the necessity of constructing a full firing range.

recognised this, remarking that pageantry's "historical interest is as much national as local."[44] Other small towns also picked up on this narrative. In St Albans, for example, one resident in 1962 remembered how, during the 1907 pageant, "[t]he ordinary citizen began to feel that there was something special about his city and something worth preserving. It was little enough, but it was the beginning of civic knowledge which leads to civic pride."[45] In Romsey, the pageant author was explicit in connecting the small town to the larger picture, arguing "It is but a step from the story of each English town, to the wider scenes and the grander Drama of our National History."[46] This connection between locality and a larger story was further encouraged during an associated sermon by Rev. A. J. Grieve, who affirmed that "[in] modern England [...] patriotism is a threefold cord, combining love of land, of country, and of town or village."[47] Into the interwar period, this ethos remained common. During Ilminster's pageant in 1927 (population approximately 2,300), for example, the *Chard and Ilminster News* suggested that

"pageants in their diversity of scene and colour appeal to the emotions of local pride, and so to a true patriotism and love of country; citizens, unconsciously almost, learn the broad facts of general history, and with aroused pride desire to carry on what is their heritage and the hallowed memory of footsteps which trod where they now tread."[48]

An active culture was a further extension of local pride. In a necessary but important contrast to larger towns and cities, the historical pageants of small towns had a much stronger element of local involvement. In Romsey, for example, over a quarter of the town's inhabitants actually served as performers.[49] In addition to cast members, pageants also required large numbers of local volunteer costume- and property-makers, stewards, stage managers and other organisers. When the numbers of those involved in such roles are added to the numbers of local people who also saw the pageant, it becomes clear that an efficient and enthusiastic civic culture was vital to mobilising the huge collective effort that pageants necessitated. As manifested in the context of pageants, this

---

44 "The Sherborne pageant," *The Times* (13 June 1905), 4.

45 Quoted in Freeman, "'Splendid display; pompous spectacle,'" 430.

46 *Romsey Millenary Celebration A.D. 907–A.D. 1907: Words and Music*, (Romsey: Mayor's Parlour 1907), 11.

47 *Hampshire Independent* (29 June 1907), 12.

48 "The Ilminster Pageant," *Chard and Ilminster News* (22 October 1927), 3.

49 *Southampton Times and Hampshire Express* (22 June 1907), 3.

civic culture was a pluralistic mode of communication and persuasion involving consensual negotiation between the different interest groups that took part, such as local associations, municipal government and churches, not to mention the many individual volunteers.[50] For the duration of a pageant this civic culture was geared towards values that emphasised the pride and identity of the small town, as well as the symbolic yet purposeful performing of the relationship between government, associational culture and the individual town-dweller. It transcended traditional political divisions, offering a shared sense of belonging rooted in the history of the place.[51]

Often, this involved a mammoth undertaking. In Newark in 1935 (population c. 20,000), for instance, each episode had between one and three production committees, each representing different societies or communities in the town – examples included the Roman Catholic and Anglican churches, the National Association of Local Government Officers, and the High School Old Girls Association. Alongside the variety of small committees – from "Horses" to "Properties" – was a large executive committee of forty-two men and women.[52] In Newark as elsewhere, the completion of the pageant was followed by a very deliberate eulogising of this civic relationship by the pageant organisers and the press. For example, at Wells in 1923 the pageant-master discoursed on the reasons for the success of the town's pageant, lauding the "spirit of teamwork," the "unfailing energy, determination and self-sacrifice on the part of the producers," and, finally, "the willing and unstinted support given by those many unnamed persons without whose co-operation the pageant could never have taken place."[53] Such declarations were common throughout the century.[54]

---

50 Gabriel A. Almond and Sidney Verba, *The Civic Culture: Political Attitudes and Democracy in Five Nations* (London: Sage Publications 1963), 6; Laura A. Reese and Raymond A. Rosenfeld, "Comparative civic culture: theory and methods." In *Comparative Civic Culture: The Role of Local Culture in Urban Policy-Making*, ed. Laura A. Reese and Raymond A. Rosenfeld (Farnham: Ashgate Publishing Limited 2012), 3–20.

51 Peter Shapely, *The Politics of Housing: Power, Consumers and Urban Culture* (Manchester: Manchester University Press 2007), 11; John Street, "Political culture – from civic culture to mass culture," *British Journal of Political Science* 24 (1994), 104.

52 "Newark Pageant," *Newark Pageant Minute Book*, Nottingham Archive: DD/NM/15/15/1; *The Pageant of Newark: Official Programme* (Newark 1936), copy in Nottingham Archive: DD /NM/15/19/45.

53 "Wells historical pageant," *Wells Journal, Somerset and West of England Advertiser* (3 August 1923), 5.

54 It is worth noting that both Mick Wallis and Michael Woods have seen such aspects of civic culture around pageantry as examples of social control, and a way to mobilise the work-

2. The themes of pageant narratives

The themes addressed in pageant narratives were designed to demonstrate how the history of the small town was important to the general history of the nation. In this way the performance of the past aimed at creating, or bolstering, a sense of pride in the present, as well as providing lessons for the future. For the Thirsk pageant in 1907, for example, the author – local vicar F. L. Perkins – argued that "[t]he history of Thirsk provides ample theme for pageantry and play [...]. From pre-Roman times Thirsk has been a town of importance, playing its part in county affairs, and helping largely in incidents that have been of national import and contributing to the country's history."[55] To support such claims, pageants adopted various stratagems. One that was particularly common was the inclusion of scenes where the small town was shown as having been honoured by the presence of important royal or ecclesiastical figures. Queen Elizabeth I was an especially popular character, pageant re-enactments of the festivities associated with her visits to localities evoking a pastoral and contented "Merrie England."[56] The final scene of the St Albans pageant (1907), for example, featured Elizabeth visiting the town in 1572, seated on a throne surrounded by lords and ladies (see Figure 2), accompanied by Morris dancing and masques; the fifth episode of the Gloucestershire pageant (1908), performed in Cheltenham, showed Elizabeth at Sherborne House in 1574, watching Morris dancing and maypole revels; and the tenth and penultimate episode of the Warwick pageant (1906) showed the queen meeting Shakespeare in the town and watching special dances. Such portrayals of previous royal visits were often linked to present-day claims to monarchical favour, so as to underline the small town's ongoing importance to wider national life. An excellent means of doing this was to solicit royal patronage. In the early twentieth century, Queen Victoria's daughter Princess Louise was an especially important source of this, visiting many pageants, including Romsey, Bury St Edmunds, and Gloucestershire.[57]

This trend continued in later years. Bridport's pageant in 1953 serves as a particularly evocative example. For many of the townspeople the

---

ing-class population behind the ambitions of civic elites. Mick Wallis, "The popular front pageant: its emergence and decline," *New Theatre Quarterly* 11 (1996), 18–19; Woods, "Performing power."

55 *The Thirsk Historical Play* (Thirsk 1907).
56 Readman, "The place of the past," 186.
57 David Duff, *The Life Story of H. R. H. Princess Louise, Duchess of Argyll*, (London 1949), 242.

Fig. 2: Queen Elizabeth I in the St Albans pageant, 1907. Used with permission of St Albans Museums.

main draw of the pageant was the visit of Princess Margaret on the opening night, scheduled long before the first performance took place – and seemingly the first "official" royal visit in the town's history.[58] To show their gratitude a "beautifully leather-bound blue souvenir programme," tooled in gold and printed on art paper – and lacking the advertisements of the normal souvenir – was presented to the Princess.[59] The fanfare accorded to Margaret underscored the purpose of the pageant, which was to commemorate the anniversary of the granting of a royal charter in 1253, and this being the case the story told was naturally dominated by the visitations of royals to Bridport in times gone by. As the *Dorset Daily Echo* pointed out, the history of Bridport was also the history of the Princess's own ancestors – "brought richly to life before her as she and her suite watched from the Royal Box."[60] Each royal figure depicted in the pageant had their own compliment to give to Bridport and Dorset, from its topography to its industry; and these appreciative remarks were duly acknowledged with cheers from the grateful townsfolk. King Athelstan, for example, said he had come to "breathe the sweetness of our Dorset air"; King John made it clear that he wished to procure Bridport rope as it was "the best in the world"; and Queen Joan of Navarre was fascinated by the crafts of the town and amused by the acrobats and tumblers dancing on the Green. Indeed, in the case of King John, a figure usually

---

58 Rodney Legg, *The Book of Bridport: Town, Harbour and West Bay* (Tiverton: Halsgrove 2003), 135.
59 "West Dorset Notes: The man behind Bridport's Charter pageant," *Dorset Daily Echo* (12 June 1953), 5.
60 "Pageant tells the history of Bridport," *Dorset Daily Echo* (24 June 1953), 8.

disparaged in pageants, his visit to Bridport redeemed him in the eyes of the citizens who, after initially viewing him with suspicion, cheered at his purchase of Bridport rope. This was partly derived from fact, at least: in 1211 the town's ropes were royally endorsed in a letter from King John to the Sheriffs of Dorset and Somerset, in which he commanded the people of Bridport to work day and night to supply the navy with ropes, cables and twisted yarns.[61]

If the royal dominance of many pageants might seem obsequious, it was not unusually so, being in line with mainstream attitudes to the monarchy, which remained a central pillar of British national identity throughout the twentieth century.[62] Furthermore, such outpourings of monarchical enthusiasm were very often accompanied by confident assertions of the governmental and economic independence of the town, usually through the granting of charters confirming municipal powers. At Bridport, many episodes concentrated on cementing the notion of the town as a place in charge of its own destiny, given independent rights from the higher power of the Crown. The first episode, for example, detailed Bridport's minting of its own coins, while the third episode described the granting of the charter in 1253 that made the town a Royal Borough, the chorus announcing how "by this Charter, aptly penned and scrolled, Their liberties for aye our heirs shall hold." The sixth episode dealt with another charter, granted by Elizabeth I in 1594, which gave the town its market rights, the chorus reminding the audience how "A market every week shall be our right, Henceforth for Bridport's profit and delight" – words written to underline the continuing importance of the market to Bridport.[63] Again, as with most pageants, civic and national pride co-existed and reinforced each other: as the *Bridport News* asserted, "it made one proud of town heritage and, because it was essentially so English, prouder still of our deep roots in this island."[64]

While, over the course of the first fifty years of the century, there were many different "types" of pageants, and different levels of seriousness or splendour in their performance, certain aspects of small-town pageantry remained constant. First, a pageant required the commitment of local

---

61   Matthew Nathan, *The Annals of West Coker* (Cambridge: Cambridge University Press 1957), 133.

62   See Jonathan Parry, "Whig monarchy, whig nation: Crown, politics and representativeness 1800–2000." In *The Monarchy and the British Nation 1780 to the Present*, edited by Andrzej Olechnowicz, (Cambridge: Cambridge University Press 2004), 47–75, esp. 65–75.

63   Alexandra Richards, *Slow Dorset: Local, Characterful Guides to Britain's Special Places* (Chalfont St Peter Bradt Travel Guides 2012), 110.

64   "It would do Britain good," *Bridport News* (26 June 1953), 10.

people and associations to ensure the success of the event: no pageant could be staged without large-scale community backing. Second, pageant narratives demonstrated the co-existence and mutual interaction of sentiments of local and national pride and identity, the historical achievements and loyalty of smaller places being portrayed as vital to the maintenance of the national whole. It has been suggested that their emphasis on the importance of local history and identity made historical pageants an anti-modern phenomenon.[65] Certainly Louis Napoleon Parker decried some aspects of recent economic and cultural change, notably the growth of brash forms of commercialism, arguing that this was "precisely the kind of spirit which a properly organised and properly conducted pageant is designed to kill. This modernising spirit, which destroys all loveliness of its own to put in its place, is the negation of poetry, the negation of romance."[66] Yet he, and other pageant masters and organisers, made extensive use of modern techniques of advertising and publicity to promote their performances, through posters, postcards, lavishly illustrated books of words, and many other souvenirs.[67] They were also enthusiastic in adopting the latest means of production to dramatise history – such as floodlighting and, increasingly in the interwar period, film and amplified music.[68]

Furthermore, the use of history in pageant narratives should not be seen as any reflection of an idea that the past was necessarily or inevitably superior to the present. The stories told in pageants reflected a belief that history was exemplary: as the Bishop of Chichester declared in the course of his sermon at the inaugural service of the Pevensey pageant in 1908, a pageant "ought to be an instruction [...] [it] bade them look back and learn, not regret."[69] Similarly, in opening the Stafford pageant in 1913, the Bishop of Lichfield declared his hope that "by such a vivid representation of Stafford's history [...] we shall be stimulated to do our part in the great

---

65 Glassberg, *American Historical Pageantry*, 149–150; Woods, "Performing power," 59. For H. V. Nelles, the Parkerian pageant "had explicit anti-modern impulses," the aim being "to combat the spirit of the age": Henry Vivian Nelles, *The Art of Nation-Building: Pageantry and Spectacle at Quebec's Tercentenary* (Toronto: University of Toronto Press 1999), 144.

66 Parker, "Historical pageants," 142–143.

67 Yoshino, *Pageant Fever*, 77–81.

68 The pageant of Parliament in 1934, for example, had amplified sound, while the Greenwich Night pageant, in 1933, used high-powered floodlighting and cut-outs to create shadow images. See *Pageant of Parliament* (London: Fleetway Press 1934), and *Book of the Pageant, Greenwich, 1933* (London: "Official Publishers" 1933).

69 *Sussex Daily News* (21 July 1908), 5.

work of the present, and be filled with greater hope for the future."[70] Inciting pageant audiences and participants "not to a mere glorying in an illustrious past, but to emulate in widely differing circumstances [...] the spirit of the achievements of their forefathers" (as the official souvenir of the 1907 St Albans pageant had it),[71] this preservation of the exemplary past was further designed to bolster a historically rooted sense of identity in the context of twentieth-century modernity. And despite Parker's strictures against the "modernising spirit," this impulse is best understood as very modern in character and function, being an adaptive response to the rapidity of contemporary technological, economic and other changes.[72] As life speeded up, maintaining affective connections to a shared past became increasingly important, particularly in places – such as small towns – that might otherwise have felt left behind by the onward sweep of change. The celebration of historical continuities gave reassurance not only of the antiquity of the locality commemorated – itself a source of pride – but of its survival and growth down the centuries, and the concomitant progress of the wider national community. Arthur Balfour, the former prime minister, made precisely this point in a speech associated with the Hertford pageant celebrations of July 1914. As the pageant demonstrated, Balfour told his audience, towns like Hertford represented progress: "There was no question of being in a backwater of life." Indeed, he went on, the "great manufacturing centres" might be important, but "if they would understand some of the most valuable elements in the social life of this country it was not to those enormous and relatively modern developments that they should look. It was rather to the steady growth and advancement of communities like their own."[73]

3. The decline of pageantry?

If the example of historical pageantry is an important corrective to assumptions of cultural decline in small towns for the Edwardian and interwar periods, it is more difficult to reappraise the postwar period in the same way. In the second half of the twentieth century, pageantry, generally, declined as a widespread and popular movement. With some

---

70   *Lichfield Mercury* (1 August 1913), 8.

71   *St Albans and Its Pageant* (St Albans 1907), 15.

72   For this context, see Stephen Kern, *The Culture of Time and Space 1880–1918*, 2nd ed. (Cambridge, MA: Harvard University Press 2003).

73   *Aberdeen Journal* (2 July 1914); *Manchester Evening News* (1 July 2014).

notable exceptions, such as Bridport in 1953 or Bury St Edmunds in 1959, small-town pageants were increasingly performed indoors to much smaller audiences, and were subsumed in wider celebrations, no longer enjoying "main event" status.[74] Gradually, at least in comparison to previous decades, they became infrequent, and no longer captured the reams of newspaper coverage they once had done. But the decline was not uninterrupted. There were some peaks in the levels of pageant activity, particularly around the Coronation of 1953, the Jubilee of 1977, and (on a much smaller scale) the Millennium celebrations of 2000. But it is fair to say that the first half of the twentieth century had seen the apotheosis of historical pageantry. In a sense, the social changes of the postwar period compounded the decline. Urban sprawl meant that small towns increasingly became dormitories, or were incorporated into commuter belts, with their rural or country identities often being subsumed into larger urban areas.[75] The continued proliferation of suburbs also had an important effect on the changing character of small towns.[76] In his 1983 study of the English county town, Russell Chamberlin described how suburbs had "diluted the town, shifting the centre of gravity from the heart of the place without providing an equivalent elsewhere." Lacking churches, pubs, shops and work, and with inadequate transport, the better living conditions could not offset the more general damage.[77] Furthermore, according to Chamberlin, the rise of "dreary, featureless urban environments" from the 1960s "totally erase[d] what had taken centuries to grow."[78]

Bury St Edmunds is indicative of the effect such social change could have on a small town's experience of and engagement with pageantry. As a town that staged three high-profile historical pageants across the century, as well as a place that experienced late urban and light-industrial growth, it provides a telling case study. The town's first pageant in 1907 was masterminded by Louis Napoleon Parker, and was wildly successful. It was performed to packed crowds over several days and made a profit of over £1,000: the *Observer* called it "a triumph in pageantry," while *The Times* described the "spectacular effects" as "perhaps the most

---

74 The Bridport pageant, or "Bridport through the ages," consisted of eight episodes, 1,300 performers and six performances – impressive considering Bridport was only a small town of about 6,200 inhabitants at this time. *Bridport Royal Charter Pageant 1253–1953*. Dorset History Centre: D.2089/5.

75 Royle, "Development of small towns," 184.

76 Ibid.

77 Eric Russel Chamberlin, *The English Country Town* (Exeter: Webb & Bower 1983), 187.

78 Ibid., 196.

Fig. 3: A scene from the Bury St Edmunds pageant, 1959. Source: Courtesy of the *Bury Free Press*, www.buryfreepress.co.uk.

splendid" Parker had yet created.[79] In 1959 Bury held a second pageant (see Figure 3), produced by Christopher Ede, the leading pageant-master of the postwar period. Another large-scale event, its thousand-strong cast put on twelve performances to sell-out audiences, and it too made a significant profit and was declared a grand success.[80] This pageant was followed, in 1970, by what was to be Bury St Edmunds's final twentieth-century pageant, "Edmund of Anglia." In common with the previous half-century of pageants, the organisers believed that "pride in our past stimulates those of the present to foster the pride of today and to work and plan for our future, so that Bury St Edmunds will continue to be a

---

79 "Bury St Edmunds' great effort," *Observer* (30 June 1907), 8; "The St Edmundsbury pageant," *The Times* (9 July 1907), 11; "Statement of accounts balance sheet: Auditor's report and certificate," file of correspondence with the Pageant organisers; application of F. T. Carter to be Pageant Secretary; papers and correspondence relating to the disposal of surplus funds (1907): Suffolk Record Office, Bury St Edmunds branch, EE500/34/1.

80 "Bury's pageant of Magna Carta made a profit of £2,158," *Bury Free Press* (30 October 1959), 1. For public reaction to the pageant, see the reports in *Bury Free Press* (12 June 1959).

centre in which it is a pleasure to work and live."[81] Unlike the previous pageants, however, it made a small financial loss. But more worrying to the organisers was the opposition it garnered. In the letters pages of the local press and in the council chamber, some townspeople complained about the high cost of the ratepayer-funded event, and the unsuitability of the content – which was wholly focused on the life of St. Edmund – for what was now seen as a modern town.[82] This groundswell of opinion culminated in the performance of an alternative puppetry pageant by a small group of rebellious local youths, lampooning the official pageant as stuffy and irrelevant, and making fun of its producer Olga Ironside Wood – or "Lady Olga-Ironside Woodentop," as they called her. While it garnered only a small audience, it was reported in the local press, and soured the finale of the pageant proper. As one of the organisers of the puppet show, Julian Putkowski, remembered in 2014,

> "There was an alternative Bury St Edmunds, populated by young late-teens and early twenty year olds during the mid to late 1960's for whom the pageant was a costly irrelevance. They weren't really party political but took umbrage at the large amount of money that was being squandered on the pageant. My principal complaint was that it was a business promotion and had damned all to do with the majority of the townsfolk and as I think I indelicately expressed it fuck all to do with folk living on Mildenhall and Howard estates. Then, and I surmise to some extent nowadays the overwhelmingly working class estate dwellers were marginalised."[83]

As Putkowski hinted, Bury St Edmunds had changed a great deal. Since the Second World War, the town had seen "a period of expansion which can only be paralleled by the twenty years between the Norman Conquest in 1066 and the compilation of Domesday Book in 1086."[84] By 1960 the building up of the Mildenhall estate was well under way, joining the Howard estate and the Nowton Road housing. Industrial estates were also built, as Bury St Edmunds actively courted London firms to come and set up under a town expansion scheme. Agriculture, while still

---

81 Olga Ironside Wood, *Edmund of Anglia* (Bury St Edmunds: privately published 1970), 3.

82 "The future is more important," *Bury Free Press* (3 July 1970), 10; "Why it was decided to commemorate," *Festival of St. Edmund* [*Bury Free Press* supplement] (3 July 1970), 2; "Anyway, who cares about Edmund? Not young set," *Bury Free Press* (10 July 1970), 12.

83 Julian Putkowski in an email to Tom Hulme, 19 June 2014. For press coverage, see *Bury Free Press* (24 July 1970), 12; *East Anglian Daily Times* (27 July 1970), 8; *Bury Free Press* (31 July 1970), 13.

84 Margaret Statham, *The Book of Bury St Edmunds* (Buckingham: Barracuda Books 1988), 127.

important, was joined in the local economy with new businesses of many kinds, from Nilfisk, the Danish vacuum cleaner manufacturers, to Vitality Bulbs and Vinten, who made specialist cameras.[85] Accordingly, the population of the town climbed sharply: after staying at around 16,000 from 1881 to 1931, it reached 20,056 in 1951 and 25,661 in 1971.[86] Inevitably, these economic and social changes, and the "blurred suburbanised vision" they represented, were not welcomed wholeheartedly: the famous historian of Suffolk, Norman Sharpe, lamented that "the extraordinary decision to double the town, from 20,000 to 40,000 is relentlessly changing both its heart and country setting."[87] In the face of such changes, the pageantry format seemed increasingly quaint and obsolete.

4. The Axbridge resurgence

Yet, if pageants seemed irrelevant to many, they retained considerable significance in certain places. Raphael Samuel brackets them with a range of manifestations of "living history" that emerged in the post-war period, especially the 1960s, including battle re-enactment, folk museums and railway preservation.[88] Notable outdoor pageants still took place from time to time, for example in Berkhamsted, Hertfordshire, in 1966, and Carlisle in 1977, and many "pageant-plays" were held indoors, with smaller casts and audiences.[89] Some small towns came late to historical pageantry: one example is the small Somerset town of Axbridge. Although it is the smallest place considered in this chapter, Axbridge fits Royle's definition of a small town: it had just over 2,000 inhabitants at the 2011 census, but has a greater "variety of functions" than a village; it is governed by a "town council." (Even in the late nineteenth century, with a population below 1,000, it was described in Bartholomew's *Gazetteer of the British Isles* as a "small town.")[90] Axbridge's first historical pageant was organised in 1967 – a surprisingly late addition to the rich tradition

85 Ibid.

86 Ibid., 140.

87 Carol Twinch, *Bury St Edmunds: A History and Celebration*, (Salisbury 2004), 82.

88 Raphael Samuel, *Theatres of Memory, Volume I: Past and Present in Contemporary Culture* (London: Verso 1994), 169–202, esp. 176, 191–192.

89 Freeman, "Splendid display; pompous spectacle," 448–449; *The Carlisle Pageant '77* (Carlisle: Cumbrian Newspapers Group 1977).

90 John Bartholomew, *Gazetteer of the British Isles* (London 1887): GB Historical GIS/University of Portsmouth, http://www.visionofbritain.org.uk/place/12349 (accessed 26. 11. 2015).

of pageantry in the West Country. The pageant was staged to celebrate the opening of the A371 Axbridge bypass, a measure that was aimed at relieving the congestion and pollution the town had suffered since the advent of the motor car.[91] It was also argued that more than thirty years' uncertainty regarding the bypass had held up the economic develop- ment of Axbridge.[92] The idea for the pageant seems to have originated in a discussion between the town clerk, Ernest Thorne, and two local women – Chris Cowap and Jocelynn Gibson. After this conversation, Thorne publicly suggested that a historical pageant detailing the town's "long and distinguished history" would be a good way to commemorate the occasion. The local press agreed, thinking that it might "get the town moving."[93] Gibson, who had experience as an actor and director, produced the pageant, while Cowap – advised by local historian Hilda Lovell – was responsible for the script.[94]

Although it came six decades after the first wave of "pageant fever," the themes and production of the Axbridge Pageant were remarkably faithful to Parker's original Edwardian vision. The costumes were most- ly made by the women of the town, in contrast to many other postwar pageants, and all the amateur actors were drawn from the locality.[95] Admission was even free (one of Parker's original stipulations that had been quickly forgotten, not least by the man himself).[96] In terms of its narrative the pageant also had a lot in common with its Edwardian fore- bears. The performance began, as so many had done, with the Roman invasion. Throughout the pageant there were scenes associating local history with nationally important people, most prominently the regal and ecclesiastical figures who had visited the town or its vicinity at some time or other, such as Kings John and Edmund, Abbot Dunstan, and Queen Henrietta Maria. The role the town and its inhabitants played in key episodes of national history, such as the English Civil War and the Monmouth Rebellion, also featured strongly. The narrative, of course, paid particular attention to the local, portraying the development of the administration and economic growth of the town, with scenes showing

---

91 Harry Mottram, "The Axbridge Pageant," *Somerset Magazine* 10, no. 8 (August 2000), 28.
92 "Pageantry in Axbridge town," *Cheddar Valley Gazette* (22 September 1967), 1.
93 Ibid.; Mottram, "Axbridge Pageant," 28.
94 "Pageantry in Axbridge town," *Cheddar Valley Gazette* (22 September 1967), 1; Hilda Lovell, "Axbridge, Somerset: History of a Domesday Borough with special reference to the develop- ment of local government," MPhil thesis (University of London, 1971). See "Research in urban history," *Urban History* 2 (1975), 154, for a brief overview of Lovell's thesis.
95 "Harking back to the good old days," *Cheddar Valley Gazette* (18 August 1967), 12.
96 Goodden, *Story of the Sherborne Pageant*, 11.

the bestowal of charters, as well as hiring fairs and the coming of the railway. It ended with the advent of the motor car in the twentieth century – a neat touch, which allowed the town to celebrate the overcoming of its former oppressor by the new bypass road.

In the month before the performance a local columnist for the *Cheddar Valley Gazette* declared the pageant to be an example of "the old spirit that was once such a feature of country life, where everyone joined to do something together" – something that "many people" had been quick to say was over.[97] Such an impression was heightened by the specific production of the pageant, with each episode being given to a local association – such as the Axbridge Youth Club, the Mendip Round Table, the Axbridge Town Trust, or the Axbridge Women's Institute.[98] With 175 performers and approximately one hundred helpers, over a quarter of the town's residents had a hand in the production.[99] And since over three thousand people watched the pageant, it is likely that a large majority of the town either took part in or saw it. As the *Cheddar Valley Gazette* claimed, it was thus a case of "a whole town really putting all its effort into making the event a success," utilising a network of local associations and a shared local history.[100]

After the dress rehearsal, which around three hundred spectators attended, excitement in the town grew: the *Gazette* predicted that "the real thing should be about the most colourful and impressive spectacle to have been seen in the town for many years."[101] A full spread, including the front page, in the edition following the pageant confirmed the newspaper's hopes, as it declared "one of the most impressive events ever to have been seen in the quaint and picturesque little community."[102] The director, Gibson, announced she was "amazed that so many inexperienced people could put on such a smart show with so little rehearsal," while Cowap, the scriptwriter, thought "Axbridge did itself proud, especially when you consider its size. Everyone pulled together and it was a marvellous thing to be involved in. The people taking part absolutely surpassed themselves."[103] With a tripling of the town's population for the day and intense local enthusiasm the pageant was, then, a significant success.

---

97 "Harking back to the good old days," *Cheddar Valley Gazette* (18 August 1967), 12.

98 "Highlights from the history of an ancient royal borough presented by the people of Axbridge and district," Somerset Heritage Centre, PAM 89.

99 "Pageantry in Axbridge town," *Cheddar Valley Gazette* (22 September 1967), 1.

100 Ibid.

101 "Pageant rehearsal 'success'," *Cheddar Valley Gazette* (15 September 1967), 1.

102 "Pageantry in Axbridge town," *Cheddar Valley Gazette* (22 September 1967), 1.

103 Ibid.

Indeed, the extent of its triumph was underlined by the decision, just three years later, to stage another pageant in the town. Again simply named the "Axbridge Pageant", the 1970 performance was timed to coincide with the town's twinning with Houlgate in France.[104] As in 1967, it was directed by Jocelynn Gibson, this time aided by Anne Cannon (though on the day Gibson was prevented from taking part due to illness).[105] In terms of narrative and themes, the pageant was a direct replica of the 1967 event.[106] The number of performers had grown, however, from 175 in 1967 to 250 in 1970. In the text of the programme the history of the town's fabric was given particular attention, a case being made for its lasting architectural importance: "In our streets and buildings our history is visible. The lay-out of the town is still essentially medieval [...] in an age of sprawling housing estates and shopping-centres all looking much alike, we are fortunate to have retained the individuality and coherence of a little Somerset town that was old when the Normans came."[107] The pageant sought to bring to life the historical importance of the town, against the backdrop of this architectural heritage.

Like that of 1967, the 1970 pageant proved a success, with over 2,000 people turning up to watch. The memory of the event was also given a boost with the production of a half-hour colour film, available for hire at £2, with a reduction for schools and charitable organisations. The *Cheddar Valley Gazette* was, of course, supportive and complimentary about the pageant describing it as "spectacular," with "vivid colour and bold action."[108] Again, the pageant captured the attention of the town, with "every family in Axbridge" represented in its production, according to one report.[109] After a surprising beginning in 1967, therefore, pageantry in Axbridge continued as a significant element of local historical culture. Indeed, the pageant was once again performed in 1980. This was, at the time, the largest staging of the pageant, now with two performances and a significantly bigger cast. In comparison to the 1967 and 1970 pageants it seems to have been slightly more commercialised: a grandstand was now erected, with tickets no longer free, and the pur-

---

104 Mottram, "Axbridge pageant," 1.
105 "Axbridge prepares for an historic weekend: Pageant and twinning," *Cheddar Valley Gazette* (18 September 1970), 1.
106 Ibid.
107 See the digitised leaflet at http://79.170.40.33/beewhizz.co.uk/Pageant/Minibooklet.gif (accessed 3. 11. 2014).
108 "History created and recreated in Axbridge pageant," *Cheddar Valley Gazette* (25 September 1970), 1.
109 Ibid.

pose of "raising much-needed money for restoring the parish church of St. John the Baptist" featured in the press and in the programme, alongside the aim of placing the town "firmly on the map." Sponsorship was garnered from local businesses, as well as from more grass-roots fundraising efforts.[110] Other commercial events were run alongside the pageant, most notably a "Made in Axbridge"-themed "country fayre" organised by Axbridge Church Enterprises, at which local products were sold. Despite such innovations, however, most of the original ethos of the pageant remained. The majority of costumes were again made by local women, and the expense of those that were hired out fell on the performers themselves.[111] As with the previous two pageants, the direc- tor declared the event a success ("Everyone was so happy and it was a super experience"),[112] and lauded the "whole pageant" as "an exercise in community spirit and co-operation" – sentiments very much in line with established traditions of pageantry.[113] Local opinion agreed. The *Cheddar Valley Gazette* described the pageant as a "mammoth extravaganza of Ax- bridge's life past and present," coming after "months of pageant fever,"[114] while the *Weston Mercury* thought "the main ingredient of success was the strong community spirit."[115]

1980 was not the end of the story, however. 1990 saw yet another Axbridge pageant, with the cast further enlarged, the number doubling to 600. In addition, the pageant was extended from two to three perfor- mances, a proper grandstand was built, and over 4,000 people saw the show – a sell-out crowd.[116] The accompanying programme of events for the pageant also grew. It included a "Songs of Praise"-style service, at which many of the congregation wore their costumes; a festival of flow- ers in the parish church, reflecting the themes of the pageant scenes; an exhibition in a local pub of painted caricatures of pageant performers; and a public dance in the town square, complete with jazz band, fol- lowing the final performance. The funds raised by the pageant and its associated events were put towards the cost of the next planned pageant in 2000 – an aim that was assisted by favourable coverage in the local

---

110 "Axbridge ready for mammoth pageant," *Cheddar Valley Gazette* (14 August 1980), 1.
111 Ibid.
112 "Crowd enjoys Axbridge's big pageant," *Cheddar Valley Gazette* (28 August 1980), 1.
113 "Axbridge gets ready for pageant 1980," *Cheddar Valley Gazette* (21 August 1980), 1.
114 "Axbridge ready for mammoth pageant," *Cheddar Valley Gazette* (14 August 1980), 1; "Crowd enjoys Axbridge's big pageant," *Cheddar Valley Gazette* (28 August 1980), 1.
115 "Axbridge relives its long history," *Weston Mercury, Somerset and Avon Herald* (29 August 1980), 1.
116 "Visitors flock to pageant," *Somerset Express* (30 August 1980), 90.

Fig. 4: A scene from the Axbridge pageant, 2010. Source: Photograph by Chris Loughlin; used with author's permission.

broadcast media and a video recording of one of the performances, which was released for sale after the event.[117] The *Cheddar Valley Gazette* was, as usual, exceedingly enthusiastic, describing the town's now well-embedded pageant as "spectacular" and a "ten-yearly extravaganza."[118] Indeed such was the self-assurance in the town's enthusiasm for its relatively newfound enthusiasm for pageantry that, on the final night, a giant open air party was held in the Square, with a jazz band and dancing, as everyone "joined the Pageant chairman in this final public duty – a toast to Axbridge Pageant 2000."[119]

5. Conclusion

Historical pageants were an important part of small-town civic culture for a large proportion of the twentieth century. Despite the supposed decline in local feeling and autonomy, amateur casts of many hundreds,

---

117 Ibid.; "Axbridge pageant – August 25, 26, 27, 1990" – unknown newspaper cutting on Axbridge pageant website, http://79.170.40.33/beewhizz.co.uk/Pageant/Scan_1990a.gif (accessed 3. 11. 2014).

118 "Town's march of time," *Cheddar Valley Gazette* (30 August 1990), 24.

119 Ibid.

and sometimes even thousands, came together in one common endeavour. Pageants depended not only on the willing actors, but a whole host of other individuals and local associations as well, who organised the pageant and helped make it happen – whether by making props and costumes, assisting with the stage management, or ensuring attendance through advertising and publicity work. These community performances were, above all, examples of small-town civic culture in action. At the same time, pageants altered and performed sweeping narratives of history, placing the small town at the forefront of patriotism and civic duty. Sometimes with considerable subtlety, these stories demonstrated the linkages between past and present, and made claims about the continued ability of small towns to meet the challenges of the future.

However, despite the resilience of historical pageants until at least the 1950s, it is undeniable that the popularity of the movement began to ebb in following decades, and never truly recovered. There are a whole host of reasons for this decline. At the most simple level, the rise of other forms of entertainment, such as television, provided an alternative draw. As Christopher Ede was already explaining in 1957 when staging the Guildford pageant, he had changed his pageant style to feature short snappy episodes, because "a public brought up on the cinema – and now on television – can scarcely bear to look at one incident for much more than ten minutes."[120] It is probable that this problem only increased as the medium grew in popularity. At the same time, other forms of local theatre sprung up to replace pageants, which were expensive and time-consuming in comparison. Ede, for example, began to pioneer "son et lumière" performances for civic events. This type of light and sound entertainment had first been presented at Chambord, France, in 1952; it was first performed in Britain in 1958. As with the original Edwardian pageants, the appeal of son et lumière rested "very much on the site" of the performance, but rather than having actual actors, the show consisted solely of music, narration, and lights.[121] Over the last twenty years of his career, Ede went on to produce many more such events, leaving historical pageantry behind him.[122]

The community play, which emerged in the 1970s and 1980s, was not usually presented as a successor in the pageant tradition, but it also served a similar purpose. Certainly, it shared many features with the

---

120 "Borough frowned upon its 'creckett' pioneer," *Manchester Guardian* (8 May 1957), 7.
121 "Buxton's light and sound pageant," *Buxton Advertiser Herald* (21 March 1958), 1; *The Pageant of Buxton in Light and Sound* (London 1958), copy in Matlock local studies library; Samuel, *Theatres of Memory*, 179–180.
122 "Obituary: Christopher Ede," *The Stage* (25 February 1988), 29.

older theatrical form: it focused on the community's history, relied on professional producers working with local amateur actors, and aimed to raise community consciousness.[123] More generally, the socio-economic and cultural changes that were starting to become apparent in the inter-war period continued. Extensive suburbanisation and the rise of central government between the 1940s and 1960s, for example, led to a decline of local government power, as the old systems of municipal government were "recast" into "a structure that, as its proponents thought, fitted a commuting rather than community-based generation."[124]

Explaining the decline of historical pageantry and accounting for the relative importance of each of these factors, is a task that remains fully to be undertaken. But, despite these long-term trends of decline, it should be remembered that small-town pageantry has not completely disappeared. Performed as planned in 2000 and again in 2010 (see Figure 4), with continued success, the example of Axbridge demonstrates the role that local traditions such as pageants can still play in revitalising small towns.[125] Axbridge, after all, did not have a pageantry tradition before 1967, and yet, since that date, the pageant has become important to the town's image, growing in strength and popularity with each staging. It is indicative of the lasting memory of pageantry as a unique cultural form, yet also its suitability to different purposes, that a "Historical Pageant seemed a natural choice" to celebrate something as modern as a new bypass road.[126] The pageant mobilised the community behind a common cause, presenting a shared past to mark the most recent development in the economic and social history of the town; moreover, its regular performance at ten-year intervals has served to establish a tradition of pageantry as an important element of the community's collective memory. In this sense Axbridge illustrates how pageants have both commemorated the pasts of localities, and also become a valued part of the histories of the same localities. Historians have recently started to give more concerted attention to historical pageants, and have encouraged small-town communities to involve themselves in remembering not only their history but also the past performances of that history.[127] For, quite apart from its

---

123 Neil Beddow, *Turning Points: The Impact of Participation in Community Theatre*, edited by Mary Schwartz, (Bristol, n.d. [2001]), 10.

124 Chandler, *Explaining Local Government*, 184.

125 See http://www.axbridgepageant.org.uk/ (accessed 29. 11. 2015).

126 "Pageantry in Axbridge town," *Cheddar Valley Gazette* (22 September 1967), 1.

127 Our project is in the vanguard of this effort. We are running local exhibitions about historical pageants, recording oral histories of pageanteers, giving local history talks and presenting film

survival as a dramatic form, the memory of historical pageantry has also survived, providing a focus for community spirit and civic culture in the twenty-first century.

---

evenings, and curating a large online presence for historical pageants. See *The Redress of the Past: Historical Pageants in Britain, 1905–2016*, www.historicalpageants.ac.uk (accessed 19. 4. 2017).

"The architectural rhythm of a small town ... is very familiar to us." A Small Town as an Aesthetic Ideal of the Twentieth Century[1]

Martin Horáček

1. Introduction

The Czech Lands (today the Czech Republic) belong among those state units (or countries) with an extraordinarily high number of small municipalities.[2] Only in the capital city of Prague does the population exceed one million, and only three other cities (Brno, Ostrava and Plzeň) have more than 150,000 inhabitants. Historiographical research into cities in the Czech Lands inevitably means research be primarily into small towns. Professional interest in these settlements in terms of architectural composition and the history of building development has quite a rich tradition. It began in the last decades of the Hapsburg Monarchy at the turn of the 19th century, and in communist Czechoslovakia it probably reached its greatest intensity from the 1950s to the 1980s. Research interest was motivated especially by heritage considerations, because the vast majority of small towns in the region had medieval origins and included a larger or a smaller fund of historically or artistically significant building structures. Architectural-historical and composition analyses, however erudite, actually seemed to substitute for the lack of any real preservational maintenance in cities and had only a limited impact on

1   The presentation of the first version of this study has been made possible through a scholarship from the Czech Association for Urban Studies and a grant from the European Social Fund (CZ.1.07/2.2.00/28.0075). Many thanks to Kathleen Brenda Geaney for her help with the English translation and to Kimberly Elman Zarecor for her comments on the work of Jiří Kroha.
2   Cf. Stanislav Balík, "Problematické institucionální stránky české místní samosprávy" [Problematic Institutional Issues of Czech Local Administration], *Kontexty* 7, no. 5 (2015), 28–34. http://www.cdk.cz/casopisy/kontexty (accessed 15. 4. 2017).

their appearance and further development.[3] With this in mind, it is not surprising that an academic study mapping the interest in small Czech towns in terms of sources of inspiration for the new architecture of the 20th century has not yet come into being. This text therefore can be considered as one of the initial steps toward such a synthesis.

2. Small Towns in Urban Planning of the Twentieth Century – an Overview

The twentieth century seemed to be an unfavourable period for small towns. An enormous increase in population, the development of a global economy, and a political ideology calling for "progress" and "modernisation" could not be reconciled with a life based in a small social and urban space. There has always been a gap between small and large settlements in terms of their forms and lifestyle. In ancient times, the Middle Ages and the early modern age, it was possible to count on one hand the number of cities with populations over one million (Rome, Constantinople, Beijing, Tenochtitlan), and there were not even many cities with populations in the hundreds of thousands (Paris, London, ports in the Mediterranean). With the arrival of the Industrial Revolution, the gap widened. Centres of production and trade functioned like large planets. Their gravitational force attracted people, capital and a system of roads, while small towns were literally and figuratively "pushed aside." Large cities were full of life, whereas small ones were sinking into oblivion.

Also in terms of the architectural profession, small towns offered much less than large cities. Buildings of higher significance and richer artistic decor were built in large cities. Schools of architecture were also located there. It was easier to secure contracts and find an audience more accommodating of a personal creative approach to design.

However, architecture is not a discipline which transforms easily or straightforwardly, or one that depends mostly on its own internal concerns. Opinions were voiced even before the twentieth century that a person could earn a lot of money in large cities, but one could not live a good life there. People would suffer psychologically and socially (ano-

---

3   Among others Oldřich Dostál et al., *Československá historická města* [Czechoslovak Historic Towns and Cities] (Prague: Orbis 1974). – For international readers especially *International History of City Development* 7: *Urban Development in East-Central Europe: Poland, Czechoslovakia, and Hungary*, Erwin Anton Gutkind, (New York – London: Free Press Collier-Macmillan 1972).

nymity), in terms of their health (a polluted environment), morally (the concentration of crime) and aesthetically (monotonous and unattractive surroundings). The alternative might be to live in a secluded place or in a village. To the majority of reformers, however, this option seemed to be lacking socially and culturally. But the small town offered an optimal and historically proven platform for the fulfilment of individual and collective needs. The questions that resonated with architects were, where a small town like this should properly be located and what it should look like. On one hand, it should function on its own as an independent organism and on the other it should not lose its connection with the centre or its professional inhabitants who depend on the metropolitan region for business.

The arguments against large cities suggest that representatives of various professions entered into discussion on the advantages of small towns, and that the line of reasoning given in their favour did not stem from the same motivational traits. Not even the defence of small towns can be unequivocally characterised as conservative, or contra-traditionalist; the former and the latter could be applied concurrently. Such ambiguity can also be observed in an in-depth discussion on the architectonic conception of small towns in the twentieth century, which is the subject matter of this study.

At the beginning of the twentieth century, two basic architectural conceptions among the supporters of small towns were popular: (a) a garden town or suburban area, and (b) a type, which did not have a set denomination and could be called a traditional picturesque small town. When referring to popularity, we mean real popularity among the public at large and not just among architects and connoisseurs of architecture. Projects for garden towns appeared occasionally as early as the eighteenth and nineteenth century. It was normal for garden towns to place residential units in family houses with gardens intended for agricultural supply, or recreation, or both. Thanks to the English author Ebenezer Howard (1850–1928), it was at the beginning of the twentieth century, when the "garden town" was given the form of a programme and almost became a political movement. According to Howard, metropolises were to be surrounded by a ring of garden towns with a limited area and a compact pre-designed plan. The construction and administration of these towns would depend on the collaboration of the community, and their form would be in accordance with the character of the landscape with no disharmonising or contrasting elements. Garden towns more or less following Howard's ideal and emerging in the Anglo-American world quickly spread into continental Europe and before WWI even into Latin America and the colonies.[4]

The second version of actualisation of the small town most likely originated in central Europe and found its full support in the Heimatschutz movement, the movement for the protection of the homeland. What was it about? The former Holy Roman Empire was a decentralised state with a large number of local metropolises which were in fact only moderately populated and with an enormous number of small towns located at the connecting lines between centres. Many of these towns managed to escape industrialisation and the subsequent transformation of their image; they were spared new dominant factories and rings of residential suburban areas with multi-storey blocks of flats. Sensitive observers suddenly started to discover the "beauty" of those forgotten small towns. They would point out their picturesque composition in the landscape, their artistically powerful outlines, the variable town interiors that offered many pleasant experiences, and the easy access to recreation in nature. These towns, they said, should be spared significant changes not only as historical documents or to please the eye, but also as examples for future construction. The most significant texts published on this topic were written by the Austrian architect and urban planner Camillo Sitte (1843–1903) and the German painter, architect and designer Paul Schultze-Naumburg (1869–1949), the first chairperson of the Heimatschutz Association in Germany (1904–1913). In his book, *City Planning According to Artistic Principles* (first published in 1889), Sitte emphasised the fact that it was in the interest of society that citizens did not become neurotic about the ugliness of the city and, in this sense, traditional towns were better than new constructions.[5] In his series of books, *Kulturarbeiten* (1901–1917), Schultze-Naumburg confronted the images of old buildings with new ones from the second half of the nineteenth century, and applied Sitte's logic to all "cultural works," including all man-made interventions in the world (towns, roads, quarries, adjustments of waterways, etc.).[6]

---

4   Ebenezer Howard, *To-morrow: A Peaceful Path to Real Reform* (London: Swan Sonnenschein & Co 1898); Robert A. M. Stern, David Fishman and Jacob Tilove, *Paradise Planned: The Garden Suburb and the Modern City*, (New York: The Monacelli Press 2013).

5   Camillo Sitte, *Der Städte-Bau nach seinen künstlerischen Grundsätzen*, 3rd ed. (Wien: Carl Graeser & Co. 1901); *Kunst des Städtebaus: Neue Perspektiven auf Camillo Sitte*, ed. Klaus Semsroth, Kari Jormakka and Bernhard Langer (Wien, Köln and Weimar: Böhlau 2005).

6   Paul Schultze-Naumburg, *Kulturarbeiten* I–IX (München: Kunstwart 1901–1917); Norbert Borrmann, *Paul Schultze-Naumburg 1869–1949: Maler – Publizist – Architekt* (Essen: Richard Bacht 1989).

These ideas appeared to be both nostalgic and futuristic. Neither Sitte nor Schultze-Naumburg aimed at heritage conservation as we understand it today. They perceived older small towns as organisms that were more viable than modern metropolises. The arguments of the Heimatschutz movement strongly emphasised ecology. They were motivated by the desire to sustain the physical and psychological health of citizens, as well as biodiversity in the environment. Schultze-Naumburg himself was not an enemy of industrial buildings, but he wanted to improve the way they looked. At the same time, he disliked the historicist styles of the nineteenth century and he was one of the pioneers of Art Nouveau. In practice, the theory of a picturesque town usually accorded with the theory of a garden town, despite the fact that the roots of both ideas were different. Many new neighbourhoods were built, comprising single-family houses or duplexes with gardens that grew somewhat organically into ensembles. They had curved streets, vistas that terminated at church spires and public buildings, and verdant public green space. Most often they were in Germany and Switzerland, but also in France, Italy, Poland, and the Czech Lands.[7]

The ideal of a small town was suppressed after WWII mostly for political and ideological reasons. The Heimatschutz movement had discredited itself by promoting Nazism. After the war, modernist architects applied industrialisation and standardisation to the construction industry, which led to residential satellites which tried to keep the image of a "green suburban area," but lacked an elaborated hierarchical aesthetic structure and the rich functional content fostered by their interwar predecessors. Furthermore, the increase in automobile usage collided with the closed compositions in terms of volume originally designed for pedestrians. Instead of looking for a compromise, architects tended to marginalise pedestrians and turned the former polyfunctional public spaces into mere roads. Today the supporters of the so-called New Urbanism fight for a remedy and the rehabilitation of the small-town ideal, and since the 1990s their voice has become stronger and more zealous. Their arguments are based on the theses of Howard, Sitte and Schultze-Naumburg and on the fact that small towns do not represent a social experiment which would be outside reality as was the case with collective houses and communist housing estates. The proof is that the

---

7 Sigrid Hofer, *Reformarchitektur 1900–1918: Deutsche Baukünstler auf der Suche nach dem nationalen Stil* (Stuttgart and London: Edition Axel Menges 2005); Elisabeth Crettaz-Stürzel, *Heimatstil: Reformarchitektur in der Schweiz 1896–1914* (Frauenfeld, Stuttgart and Wien: Huber 2005).

well-planned garden towns from the first half of the twentieth century are one of the most sought-after addresses on the real estate market.[8]

3. Zdeněk Wirth and the Attitude to Small Towns in the Czech Lands since the End of the Hapsburg Monarchy until the Communist Era

Though it had its own specifics, the situation in the Czech Lands (comprised of historical regions of Bohemia, Moravia and Silesia) followed the same general development.[9] Camillo Sitte made several urban plans especially for Moravian towns, and his book was very well known here despite the fact that it was translated into the Czech language in 1995. The *Heimatschutz* enjoyed a great reception in both major nations of the Czech Lands. In 1904, Svaz českých spolků okrašlovacích v království českém [the Union of Czech Embellishing Associations] was established in the Kingdom of Bohemia (and ceased to exist in 1951). It united many local civic associations, and from its very beginning it published the journal *Krása našeho domova* [The Beauty of Our Home]. Following the German example, the Union renamed itself Svaz českých spolků pro okrašlování a ochranu domoviny v Čechách, na Moravě a ve Slezsku [Union of the Czech Associations for Embellishing and Protecting our Homeland in Bohemia, Moravia and Silesia] in 1909. The highest number of member associations – 402 – was reached in 1913. Moreover, both German and Czech tourist associations also engaged in the protection of the homeland. Regardless of the Czech or German language majority, a strong local patriotism prevailed in small towns. This patriotism was usually fostered by an educated elite including teachers, writers and regional scholars who emphasised the specific artistic character of a given settlement and tried to raise the public awareness in order to protect it. However, not everything could be protected. For example, apart from rare exceptions, wooden houses had been completely destroyed in the nineteenth century. This was mainly due to the fact that public opinion perceived a wooden house as a sign of poverty and the owners of such a

---

8   Andres Duany, Elizabeth Plater-Zyberk and Robert Alminana, *The New Civic Art: Elements of Town Planning* (New York: Rizzoli 2003); *New Urbanism and Beyond: Designing Cities for the Future*, ed. Tigran Haas (New York: Rizzoli 2008).

9   Martin Horáček, *Za krásnější svět: Tradicionalismus v architektuře 20. a 21. století* [Toward a More Beautiful World: Traditionalism in Architecture of the 20th and 21st Centuries] (Brno: Barrister & Principal and VUTIUM 2013).

house were simply embarrassed about it. However, top-level architects as well as academic historians and architectural theorists favoured urban patterns derived from small towns. Some of them made almost no distinction between a village and a small town and were happy to get inspiration for their new design from both, while others drew a rather sharp line between those two environments.

The first group favoured traditional styles in architecture in general, while the latter tried to fabricate a new "style of our time" that was supposed to merge with the urban tissue of small towns. Local architects discussed the topic occasionally in their published writings. Dušan Jurkovič (1868–1947) might be considered the most important follower of the traditional approach, while Jan Kotěra (1871–1923) was a leader and teacher of the second, modernist group.[10] Since the modernist movement eventually prevailed, evolving from Belle Époque until the post-WWII period with only minor slowdowns, our focus here has turned to it. Regarding the potential of small towns, the most explicit statements are to be found in texts written by Zdeněk Wirth, an influential architectural historian, theorist and critic (1878–1961). [Fig. 1] He was confident that "the whole rural class was in isolation from other classes" up until the seventeenth century, and that "in terms of material supply, it was a very poor culture," and that it was only the aristocratic and ecclesiastical Baroque culture "which brought a farmer to adopting what we now call folk art." According to Wirth, in the period between the eighteenth century and the first half of the nineteenth century, townspeople tried to cultivate rural people. Then they stopped, and decided to leave rural people at the mercy of the market. That is the reason why in Wirth's times a village did not have the former "scent and purity" anymore, but instead "several poor imitations of villas and blocks of flats and many most stereotypical houses with asbestos cement roofing and intolerable windows and doors. That is the folk art of today."[11] Wirth's contempt could partly stand for a message from the so-called Vienna school of art history – one of the key representative of which was Max Dvořák (1874–1921) of Czech origin, who spoke of "unified cultural development" and put aside "social classes," which until the nineteenth century "did not actively contribute to it."[12]

10   Dana Bořutová, *Architekt Dušan Samuel Jurkovič* (Bratislava: Slovart, 2009); *Jan Kotěra, 1871–1923: The Founder of Modern Czech Architecture*, ed. Vladimír Šlapeta (Prague: Kant 2003).

11   Zdeněk Wirth, "Selský dům" [Rural House], *Stavitel* 2, no. 11–12 (1920–1921), 141–148.

12   Max Dvořák, "Restaurierungsfragen I," Kunstgeschichtliches Jahrbuch der k. k. Zentralkommission 2 (1908) / Beiblatt für Denkmalpflege, column 1–8, quoted from Ján Bakoš, *Intelektuál*

Fig. 1: Zdeněk Wirth, architectural historian, theorist and critic (1878–1961). Source: Rudolf Chadraba et al., *Kapitoly z českého dějepisu umění* II [Chapters in Czech Art History], fig. 32, Prague: Odeon, 1987.

Zdeněk Wirth preferred the cultural environment of a small town. He deserves credit for trying to identify the formal specifics of this structure so typical of the Czech Lands. He went so far as to emphasise its urban values and to advise other architects on its specifics. *Styl* [Style], the journal of the Czech pioneers of modernist architecture edited by Wirth, dedicated one issue of its first volume in 1909 to the topic of a small town. In this issue, Wirth published his own essay titled *Stavební rhytmus malého města* [The Architectural Rhythm of a Small Town]. Just as contemporary

---

& pamiatka [Intellectual & Monument], (Bratislava: Kalligram 2004), 138; Ján Bakoš, *Discourses and Strategies: The Role of the Vienna School in Shaping Central European Approaches to Art History and Related Discourses* (Frankfurt am Main: Peter Lang 2013); Matthew Rampley, *The Vienna School of Art History: Empire and the Politics of Scholarship, 1847–1918* (University Park: Penn State University Press 2013).

Fig. 2: Sušice, a typical Bohemian small town: a historical town square with the town hall, in the background a pilgrimage church on a hill. Photo: Martin Horáček, 2011.

Western-European urban reformists did, Wirth emphasised in his article the importance of shaping volumes as opposed to the accuracy of stylistic details, and admired the "beautiful sights" of townscapes as well as the "three levels of artistic gradation" upwards, based on the height of the city walls, ordinary houses and towers. He considered "compactness and effortless understanding of the whole" to be the characteristic features. In contrast to village housing development, he saw the future of small towns in connection with the modern lifestyle as well as architectural style and, in particular, with the concept of a garden town: "The overall appearance always tends to move more toward concentration, calm and the elimination of details. It is very familiar to us and we understand it not only because it is a Czech town but because it is art which is well understood in every period. We can feel why this inherited rhythm has the right to exist even today… That is the reason why the preservation of a small town's character is such an important and responsible issue for us today in the time of upgrading small towns to large cities […]"[13] Perhaps

13   Zdeněk Wirth, "Stavební rhytmus malého města" [The Architectural Rhythm of a Small Town], *Styl* 1 (1909), 327–336.

Fig. 3: Sušice, a town square. Photo: Martin Horáček, 2011.

Fig. 4: Sušice High School designed by Ladislav Skřivánek, 1911. Photo: Martin Horáček, 2011.

Fig. 5: Sušice, Benátky and Stodůlky garden suburb by Jindřich Freiwald, 1923–1925. Photo: Martin Horáček, 2011.

the new neighbourhoods in the town of Sušice in southwest Bohemia best fulfilled Wirth's visions. In the period between 1910 and 1940, a new construction, led by talented architects such as Ladislav Skřivánek, Jindřich Freiwald and Karel Pecánek, surrounded the historical centre [Fig. 2–5].

After the sovereign state of Czechoslovakia was established in 1918, Zdeněk Wirth became the chairman of the public enlightenment department at the Ministry of Education and National Enlightenment; he ran this office from 1923 to 1938.[14] He returned to the ministry in 1945. With the transition to the communist system in 1948, he assumed other significant public roles. His true influence on Czech architecture and heritage conservation has not been thoroughly researched yet. However, his power was undoubtedly considerable. He was a recognised authority

14 Kristina Uhlíková, *Zdeněk Wirth, první dvě životní etapy (1878–1939)* [First Two Stages of Life of Zdeněk Wirth (1878–1939)] (Prague: Národní památkový ústav 2010); *Zdeněk Wirth pohledem dnešní doby* [Zdeněk Wirth in Contemporary View], ed. Jiří Roháček and Kristina Uhlíková (Prague: Artefactum 2010).

for architects whose education and eloquence were slowly deteriorating, as well as for politicians regardless of their political views or party membership.

While Wirth had high hopes for the communist regime in terms of the conservation of cultural heritage, in reality, the regime completely denied the ideal of small towns. There was no need for extensive construction, as WWII did not cause much damage in Czechoslovakia and a lot of properties became available after the expulsion of three million citizens of the German nation. "For economic and cultural reasons we therefore decided to undertake the intended reconstruction, rehabilitation and completion of towns and to reduce establishing new neighbourhoods which are not necessary in our already densely populated country,", declared architects Vilém Lorenc and Otakar Nový in 1956.[15] In 1950, the government established urban conservation areas in 30 historical town centres (22 in Bohemia and Moravia, and the rest in Slovakia). Moreover, the government made a commitment to renew all of them in a period of ten years at state expense, private properties included. In 1956, the parliament of Czechoslovakia passed Act No. 40/1956 providing for state natural protection and finally in 1958, Cultural Heritage Act No. 22/1958. Thus the protection of solitary monuments and selected areas was formally secured and given the highest level of support which was never reached in any of the previous regimes.

Forty years later, there were 1.2 million flats (almost one-third of the whole number, according to the 2001 census) in cuboid structures of high-rise blocks in the Czech Lands. They were artistically poor (just a few types differing in size and layout with unified right-angled structures), energy-intensive (enormous heat losses) and time-consuming in terms of construction (in comparison with Ferro concrete constructions with the shuttering built at construction sites). In 1956, the government passed a regulation providing for the demolition of abandoned immovable properties in order to prevent an alleged blight on the landscape and to guarantee the safety of citizens. In the following four years, the biggest demolition in the history of the country took place. Upon the order of local authorities, the army blasted away houses and whole villages in the borderlands. Approximately one thousand villages were razed to the ground. The heritage status saved urban conservation areas from radical transformation. The exception was Horní Slavkov, where a large

---

15 Vilém Lorenc et al., *Rekonstrukce historických měst* [Reconstruction of Historical Towns] (Prague: SÚRPMO 1956), 48.

part of its historical buildings was gradually demolished, so the blanket protection lost its purpose. Because of a seam of coal, over eighty settlements were demolished in north-western Bohemia. Among them was the city of Most with its compact and historically and architectonically rich centre. Such destruction had no comparison in other parts of the world.[16]

Regarding new family houses, only an insignificant number of them were built in the 1950s and 1960s. The government which had become the sole constructor preferred prefabricated blocks of flats with a large capacity of housing units. These were heavily decorated in the Stalin era while in the Khrushchev era there was no decoration other than a right-angled panel grid on the surface. Many architects considered such development to be a success and the realisation of the dream of better architecture for a seemingly better communist society. Karel Janů (1910–1995) and Jiří Voženílek (1909–1986), two architects of the time and members of the pre-war architectonic avant-garde group, particularly struggled for an industrialisation and standardisation of construction. In the new regime, they assumed influential managerial positions. The former became the director of the state united construction monopoly of Czechoslovak construction companies, while the latter became the director of Stavoprojekt – a state united architectural design office which absorbed design studios that had been independent until then.[17] In communist countries, the stylistic turn in architecture from traditionalist language to modernism, which was ordered by Nikita Khrushchev, was widely welcomed by domestic architects. They perceived this change as a return to pre-war modernistic trends, and therefore, as a return to something that they had mastered and considered to be natural.

4. Architect Jiří Kroha

Quite surprisingly, it was Jiří Kroha (1893–1974), a convinced Communist and one of the most original representatives of the interwar architectonic avant-garde, who heaped criticism on the new constructions [Fig. 6]. He was in a prominent position. In the period from 1948 to

---

16 Martin Horáček, *Za krásnější svět*, 261–264, 414; Karel Kibic and Aleš Vošahlík, *Památková ochrana a regenerace historických měst v České republice 1945–2010* [Heritage Protection and Renovation of Historical Towns of the Czech Republic 1945–2010] (Prague: Národní památkový ústav 2011).

17 Kimberly Elman Zarecor, *Manufacturing a Socialist Modernity: Housing in Czechoslovakia 1945–1960* (Pittsburgh: University of Pittsburgh Press 2011).

Fig. 6: Jiří Kroha, architect and architectural critic (1893–1974).
Source: Aleš Dupal, Václav Roštlapil. *Pamětní tisk u příležitosti osmdesátých narozenin národního umělce Jiřího Krohy* [Memorial Printed on the Occasion of 80th Birthday of Nation's Artist Jiří Kroha], Brno, KSSPPOP, 1973.

1950, he was the rector of Brno University of Technology. Apart from his new roles and titles, the new regime provided him with a freedom to create that no other architect had. He even had his own studio in Stavoprojekt. However, in 1956, after he was professionally and morally denounced by a former employee, the studio was dissolved. Though Kroha lost his prominent position and actual power over architectural activities, the government let him enjoy the position of a pampered classic with the right to freely express himself at will. He was awarded the prestigious Order of Work in 1957, and a year later the Cabinet of the National Artist Jiří Kroha was founded by the Ministry of Education and Culture which became the workplace of Kroha as Chief Advisor for Issues of State Heritage and Preservation. Having this position, Kroha became a pioneer in a new approach to conservation policy, and fought fiercely to promote the preservation of architectural landmarks from the nineteenth and twentieth century that had been previously ignored. His other activities from the late period of his life involved organising his own previous work, writing a book about Soviet avant-garde and commenting on architectural affairs.[18]

Kroha had gone through an interesting style development: he was a cubist and futurist in the 1910s and 1920s, a functionalist in the 1930s, and he pursued socialist realism in the first half of the 1950s [Fig. 7]. In this particular style he even designed a whole new town, Nová Dubnica in Slovakia (1951–1957). Nevertheless, it was not the return to modernistic artistic language that bothered him, but its trivial and primitive form. He believed in architecture as an individual art and protested against the architecture of the production line.

Kroha published his opinions on architecture intensively from his youth.[19] He had expressed his reservations with regard to panel housing estates in several essays already in the 1950s; however, the most elaborated criticism seemed to appear in the *Doslov* [Afterword], dated 1965 and dedicated to the book *Nové zónování* [New Zoning] written by another prominent Czech architect Bohuslav Fuchs.[20]

Kroha's criticism is vague and glutted with phrases from communist newspeak. According to him, the problem is not the regime but the fact that planning is approached in a "formalist" and "simplified" manner. However, (given the particular situation) the objectives and recommended methods to achieve them seem revolutionary; it is socialist "humanism" which planning supposedly reaches through sociology. Without it, "many facilities of our environment get [...] into a conflict with basic [...] needs," which, according to the author, obstructs the personal development of citizens as well as their loyalty to the system.

18 *Jiří Kroha (1893–1974): Architect, Painter, Designer, Theorist: A 20th-Century Metamorphosis*, ed. Marcela Macharáčková (Brno: Muzeum města Brna 2007).

19 Cf. Kroha's bibliography in the book quoted in note 18.

20 Jiří Kroha, "Doslov: Socialistická vazba městských sídel se životním prostředím" [Afterword: The Communist Connection between Cities and the Environment, 1965], in Bohuslav Fuchs, *Nové zónování – urbanistická tvorba životního prostředí z hlediska sídelního a krajinného* [New Zoning – Urban Planning of the Environment from the Standpoint of Sites and Landscape] (Prague: Academia 1967), 84–95. All the following quotations are taken from this essay, which, unfortunately, was not included in the author's bibliography mentioned in the previous note.

Fig. 7: Jiří Kroha, Faculty of Medicine, Palacký University Olomouc, 1950–1961. Photo: Martin Horáček, 2008.

He observes "physical and psychological consequences which are apparent in the undesirable instability of economic, ideological and moral attitudes, and not just in a meaningless part of our society." We have condemned the old without replacing it with something new and better: "Construction which was functionally and visually of poor quality and which later on reflected the life style of people [...] resulted in the formation of psychological mentalities that were unknown to socialist culture till then. Helpless assimilation to the novelties of progress that were of poor quality and dysfunctional created a paradoxical relationship with seemingly abandoned values and relics of the past, a relationship that was secret on the surface though constantly present in people's minds." Monuments that were to pose as museum reminders of glorious victory over the past, turned into symbols of golden old times: "Surviving historical artistic forms of political and ideological abandoned values and relationships [...] in the everyday confrontation of the public with the non-emotional form and the poor functional quality of the majority of our socialist constructions triggered increasingly depressing rather than life-exciting aspects." Apart from "humanism," Kroha also uses other terms from traditionalist vocabulary such as "harmony" and "life," which he places in proportion: "Only in a harmonious environment [...] can the positive and life-empowering realisation of a human being take place." Opposed to this, the new construction led to "some kind of new mechanical spatial composition of disparate rhythm in which, paradoxically, the newest element often emitted a non-humanist anonymity, while the old one was pervaded with the pleasurable spirit of the past, giving a more humanistic impression despite decay. The gloomy effect of this psychologically pathological phenomenon is very well known to the citizens of our towns and settlements. [...] In such an environment, from which most of the traditional relationships were removed, an individual is perceived as a mere performance element that can be expressed in a number, and that is normatively determined by minimal work performance and by the specified consumption of all other life-preserving components. Such an individual is more or less an example of the pathological subjugation of a person to numerically and mechanically determined activities rather than an example of the humanistic interconnection of a person with the environment."

Kroha makes two suggestions: (a) let us not condemn "the sociology of a town, village or environment" in the name of a "dogmatising interpretation of Marxist-Leninist methodology," and let us continue with inspiring studies of the Czech interwar avant-garde; (b) we need to compare our situation with the capitalist West, which "realises the requirements of the wider working dependent classes so that [...] they represent a much higher standard of life in comparison with the past." Conversely, in Czechoslovakia "the vulgar identification of economic and technical methods with the most primitive construction and development methods took place on the one hand, and new production and construction methods though technologically simplified to the maximum on the other. The organisational principles of most of our new housing estates were architectonically standardised holotypes mainly of apartment residences with their organisation into rows which is most convenient for underground energy underground services, and with the facilities of social needs dependent on the most primitive forms of distribution." These housing estates are monotonous and they lack a "specific physiognomy" as opposed to the old towns. When Kroha explains what he means by that, he appears to be referring to the theory of empathy: "Environmental physiognomy [...] causes an ethical relation between a person and the ethical perception of the environment (home town, home, and homeland). [...] The physiognomic face of our towns does not show architectonic or urban elements as they are but rather the life processes that are connected with them; with time the changes in people (aging) and material (patina) come to the surface. Out of this physiognomy as a humanistic source come many moral-cultural and social relationships of life traditionalism." This traditionalism cannot be removed by slogans referring to "progress." It either comes back violently or architects accept it as a sociological fact and try for a directed "symbiosis" of the old with the new.

The advantage of the Czech Lands is the non-existence of large cities. And that is why we do not find here extreme phenomena leading "some authors to be convinced of the dying out and the end of large cities" as Kroha postulates with the book of Jane Jacobs titled *The Death and Life of Great American Cities* certainly in mind.[21] However, negative tendencies spread after 1945, and the decline of architecture is not in the author's understanding separated from the devastation of the environment: "The pollution of air and natural areas [...] does not only destroy the biological but also the humanistic nourishing capacity of nature in its environmental function." Just as Wirth did a half century earlier, Kroha now suggests following the form of "medium and small" towns. Architecture should always start with a correct distribution of functions inside these structures and among them. The absence of large cities solves two serious problems: the hypertrophy of suburbs and time-consuming traffic. A village should not be sweepingly urbanised – "it should show the social respect for the traditionalist but still present character of farm people, if they want to stay connected closer to nature."

And what benefits for users will finally arise from good urban and architectural planning? Most importantly, people gain free time. How will they be able to spend it? Not only with recreation between shifts, but by developing their personal freedom with which they will all fill public spaces: "[...] socialist private as the highly cultural and spiritual counterpart of the socialist public [...] and as a free element which manifests itself distinctively in the physiognomy of a town. It is an absolute requirement also for socialist housing, the ideal of which simply cannot be a flat limited to an intimate life and basic biological human needs; it is a personal flat as a private space for the personal free culture of the socialist person."

21 Jane Jacobs, *The Death and Life of Great American Cities* (New York: Random House 1961) [Czech edition 1975].

5. Conclusion

Zdeněk Wirth and Jiří Kroha recommended that Czech architects and urbanists look for inspiration in historical small towns in their work of planning new construction. The first such appeal was published in 1909, the second almost sixty years later. What linked them together and how, on the contrary, did their views differ?

Both Wirth and Kroha were men with leadership tendencies and had ambitions to act as spokesmen for a certain architectural generation or group. Both were also able to abandon narrow professional debate, enter real politics and take on administrative functions.[22] On top of that, both men had a somewhat elitist and authoritarian character and probably sincerely believed in the success of centrally managed companies. For this reason, they likewise identified with the communist takeover in 1948. Both also wished for a new architectural language in the new era. Their partly traditionalist recommendations were therefore in no way motivated by sentiment or nostalgia. Finally, both balanced their partial disenchantment with the reality of the actual construction with a professional interest in the heritage fund.

Different accents in Wirth's and Kroha's approach to small towns reflect their different personal focus and also a shift in historical experience. Wirth was an art historian and he primarily emphasized the quality of the units of domestic small towns; he believed in their timeliness and appropriateness to the constant psychological characteristics of the Czech man. His aesthetic and regionalist accent corresponded to the priorities of the sectoral debate in the Central European area before the Great War. A new modern and national style was sought and danger was seen both in the revival of traditional morphology and ornamentation and in the unified international visual language. In this context, Wirth's ideas did not differ from the ideas of contemporary German reformists of the so-called Heimatschutz Movement mentioned in the second part of this study.

While Wirth published his text as a young representative of the emerging architectural movement, Kroha spoke from the position of a doyen evaluating his lifetime experience. As a true Communist, he spoke to the "socialist" man rather than to the "Czech" man. Above all, he

---

22 About Wirth's political opportunism Vít Vlnas, "Od šestky k trojkám" [From the Six to the Troikas], in *Proměny dějin umění: Akta druhého sjezdu historiků umění* [Changes of Art History: Proceedings of the Second Congress of Art Historians of the Czech Republic], ed. Roman Prahl and Tomáš Winter (Dolní Břežany: Scriptorium 2007), 201–208.

spoke to those who were disappointed by modernist building, whether pre-war capitalist or contemporary socialist. Wirth's recommendations had a preventive character while Kroha's were meant to lead to the rectification of the damage already done. Although Kroha dominated the historiographical method of research, he was primarily an architect; on a long-term basis, he was especially interested in sociology among the humanities. This corresponded with a different language in his critiques. He described the problem of accepting modern construction more as a sociological than as an aesthetic matter even though – in line with Wirth – he did not overlook, in the name of the collective, the psychological attitude of the individual.

Completely new was Kroha's ecological accent. Although Wirth's companions from the Embellishment Movement wrote about the threat of environmental degradation by unsightly new construction, Wirth himself, however, saw the question of a regionally specific urban form as a matter of greater urgency in 1909. He certainly did not count himself among the nationalists; however, he could not or did not want to call on his readers with a universal ecological argument that might – hypothetically – distract their focus on local Czech peculiarities. Compared to Wirth, Kroha connected the monotonous construction of prefabricated panel housing to environmental devastation quite naturally; he saw both as a consequence of a dehumanised, mechanised vision of the world. In this, he did not differ from contemporary Western critics.[23] Just as they did, he called for architecture that would fulfil individual human desires; unlike them, however, he could not visualise how exactly the users should contribute to the imagined architecture. The ideal socialist society did not represent the same thing as civil society.

6. Epilogue

Kroha's ideas were not pursued and construction in communist Czechoslovakia worsened further [Fig. 8]. At the end of the 1980s, Rostislav Švácha, an architectural historian and critic, asked local architects: "What might be done to rescue the environment of small Czech towns?"[24] The ideal of the small town came back after the fall of communism in

---

23 Alexander Mitscherlich, *Die Unwirtlichkeit unserer Städte: Anstiftung zum Unfrieden* (Frankfurt am Main: Suhrkamp 1965) [Slovak edition 1971].

24 Rostislav Švácha [an answer in a survey], in Benjamin Fragner, "Druhá zpráva o Urbanitě" [Second Report about the Urbanita Exhibition], *Technický magazín* 32, no. 1 (1989), 11.

Fig. 8: Olomouc-Povel, a high-rise housing estate from the 1980s in the former place of a demolished suburban village. Photo: Martin Horáček, 2008.

Fig. 9: Olomouc, Upper Square with the Holy Trinity Column (UNESCO World Heritage landmark since 2000) and the renovated pavement and street furniture (1995–2001). Photo: Martin Horáček, 2011.

Fig. 10: Olomouc-Neředín, urban sprawl from the 1990s. Photo: Martin Horáček, 2008.

1989. It was called for not only by the citizens who wished to move to "a green town" following the western example of the middle class, but also by some professionals.[25] Life was brought back to many old small towns thanks to lively administrations and proactive communities. While the maintenance of old buildings and existing public spaces has improved significantly, new construction is rather unrestrained and it only exceptionally reflects the visual specifics of small towns by its character [Fig. 9–10]. Is this just because of the indolence of architects, or, have they lost the ability to perceive these specifics after being exposed to decades of demolition and cover up?

---

25 Martin Horáček, Architekt Jan Vejrych ve Slaném, reformovaná česká renesance a velké stavby na malém českém městě [The architect Jan Vejrych in Slaný, the reformed Czech Renaissance and large buildings in the small Czech town]. In *Od kabaly k Titaniku: Deset studií nejen z dějin umění* [From Kabbalah to Titanic: Ten Studies not only in Art History], ed. Lubomír Konečný et al. (Prague: Artefactum 2013), 69–101.

Strategies of Manufacturing the Tourist Experience in a Small Town: Local Community and Symbolic Construction in Myshkin[1]

Greg Yudin and Yulia Koloshenko

1. Introduction

Small towns in various regions throughout the world face challenges from economic globalisation that have gradually undermined the traditional structure of production.[2] Perhaps more importantly from a sociological point of view, these challenges put significant pressure on local communities. In small towns, the density and organisation of communal life in general are closely connected to traditional modes of production. As these habitual activities become uncompetitive in rapidly changing economic environments, reproduction of the structures of the local community tends to falter.

There are convincing reasons to believe that the preservation of local community, cohesion and solidarity are crucial for the survival of small towns. In a famous essay, sociologist and philosopher Georg Simmel described life in metropolises as regulated by a blasé attitude, indifference towards the environment and supportive of individual freedom from the constraints of community. In the same text, Simmel contrasted metropolises with small towns, characterised by the power that the community possesses over members and the social control that secures cohesion and a stable communal life. Simmel argued that from a politico-sociological viewpoint the de-individualizing small town is similar to the ancient

---

1 This work was supported by the Russian Foundation for the Humanities, research grant No. 14-33-01339.
2 Paul Courtney and Andrew Errington, "The Role of small towns in the local economy and some implications for development policy," *Local Economy* 15, no. 4 (2000), 280–301.

Fig. 1: A picture on the wall of the Mouse Palace in Myshkin. Photo by courtesy of Varvara Kobyshcha.

polis.[3] Whereas metropolises tend to be mere crowds of lonely individuals, small towns are political unities capable of coherent collective action.

While subversion of communal life can be regarded as a threat to small towns across Europe, the situation is particularly grave in Russia. Under the Soviet Union, many towns were built around or gradually became completely dependent on a single factory. The abrupt cessation of manufacturing during the post-Soviet recession was followed by Russia's swift integration into the international economy, which rendered most traditional industries uncompetitive.

In this context, many Russian small towns consider the development of tourism to be their only viable solution. These ambitions rely on exploiting a town's geographical location, historical heritage and monuments, and attractive landscapes as resources to boost the tourism industry. However, the attempts of most towns to capitalise on tourism

---

3   Georg Simmel, "The metropolis and mental life." In *The Blackwell City Reader*, edited by Gary Bridge and Sophie Watson (Chichester: Wiley-Blackwell 2010), 107.

have proven to be unsuccessful. For instance, the Association of Small Russian Tourist Towns, the sole body representing small towns with well-developed tourism industries, currently has only eight member towns.

Why do such projects fail? The literature from the field of tourist studies suggests that one reason might be the inability of small towns to master the manufacturing of a tourist experience. According to various tourism scholars, a destination attractive to tourists offers the potential of a break from everyday experience and generates a feeling of authenticity.[4] However, while the theory of authenticity, in its multiple versions, explains the success of tourist enterprises, it is rather indifferent towards the preservation of communities. While it is quite feasible for a small town to develop a tourist industry capable of generating an authentic experience, the question remains as to whether this contributes to preserving the community. Even large tourist enterprises cannot be expected to assume the functions of factories and traditional industries that used to hold communities together. Indeed, the relationship between sustainable community development and tourism management has proven to be rather ambiguous. Although communities are important resources for tourism, the efficient production of tourist experiences might have no significant effect on the revitalization of a community and even harm communal life.[5] The development of tourism could turn into a risky option for small towns if it were to become an obstacle to the regeneration of the local community.

How are the conflicts and contradictions that arise in this context shaped? What are the possible solutions? How are the politics of community intertwined with tourism management in small towns?

To tackle these questions, this research considers the rare example of a successful development of tourism from scratch in Myshkin, a small Russian town of fewer than 6,000 inhabitants. Myshkin is distinguished by the absence of an historical place identity that could be relied upon for creating a tourist site. This lack makes the symbolic construction of tourism by local leaders all the more notable. This paper draws on ethno-

---

4   Dean MacCannell, "Staged authenticity: Arrangements of social space in tourist settings," *American Journal of Sociology* 79, no. 3 (1973), 589–603; John Urry, *The Tourist Gaze* (London 2002).

5   Greg Richards and Derek Hall, "The Community: A sustainable concept in tourism development?" In *Tourism and Sustainable Community Development*, edited by Derek Hall and Greg Richards (London 2000), 1–14; Sue Beeton, *Community Development through Tourism* (Collingwood 2006), 21.

Fig. 2: Myshkin. Photo: Alexander Filyuta, (CC BY-SA 3.0).

graphic fieldwork conducted in 2013, including participant observation and more than 80 in-depth interviews with local political and business leaders, initiators of the big tourist project and ordinary residents.

The development of tourism in Myshkin is first put into a broader socio-historical context. Then, concepts from tourist studies are borrowed to explain how the tactics of combining phantasy with local history have supported the commercial success of the town. This shows how the radical constructivist approach adopted in Myshkin is backed by the local community but has had an ambiguous impact on the community's integrity.

2. Small Towns: Tourism as Salvation?

Small towns, such as Myshkin, have a distinct but usually overlooked position in Russian society. Only municipalities with a population of fewer than 50,000 inhabitants are technically classified as small towns. The country has 790 such settlements, accounting for 71% of all cities. Despite the general growth of metropolises, the number of small towns in Russia doubled from 1926 to 2010, with their populations increasing by a factor of 3.4.[6] However, these settlements appear neither attractive for living in nor particularly viable. The proportion of the general population residing in small towns shrank from 35.3% to 15.9% over these eight decades. It seems that small towns have come to be viewed as a major problem by government, which tends to treat them as dysfunctional parasites demanding state investment with little or no return.[7] However, defenders of small towns believe that they occupy a strategic place in the country's life, and eliminating them would result in the 'devastation of enormous spaces' and the depopulation of large parts of Russia.[8]

The post-Soviet period has seen many small towns suffer from the effects of mono-industrialism, or dependence on one big factory which supports the entire economy and community.[9] Other small towns, such as Myshkin, had previously survived on agriculture, which underwent rapid concentration and annexation of resources by powerful holdings, rendering many traditionally farming regions uncompetitive.[10] The closing down of factories and the privatisation of land in the post-Soviet years made these towns economically vulnerable and culturally disorganised. The factories are unlikely to reopen due to the technological backwardness of the areas, infrastructural weaknesses (e.g., poor road networks) and an uncompetitive labour force. These closures have resulted in the demographic and infrastructural degradation of towns. Most importantly, after losing the factories and *kolkhozy* (collective farms) that used to be centres for the local community, the towns were deprived of an autonomous cultural life. The label "depressive towns" refers to municipalities suffering from both economic stagnation and cultural disintegration. The case of Mishelevka, a small settlement in the Irkutsk region which experienced almost total unemployment and an overwhelming problem

---

6 Georgij M. Lappo, *Goroda Rossii: Vzgliad geografa* [Russian Cities: A Geographer's View]. (Moscow: Novyi khronograf, 2012), 152.

7 For instance, former Economy Minister Elvira Nabiullina openly admitted in 2011 that supporting "economically inefficient small towns" and preventing migration to metropolises could damage economic growth by 2–3%. http://economy.gov.ru/minec/press/news /doc20111208_004 (accessed 15. 4. 2017).

8 See the reaction to the Minister's statement by the Union of Small Towns of Russia. http:// smgrf.ru/zayavlenie-soyuza-malyh-gorodov-rf (accessed 15. 4. 2017).

9 There are around 400 mono-industrial towns in Russia with nearly 16 mln. inhabitants, which amounts to approximately 25% of the total Russian population.

10 Michele L. Crumley, *Sowing Market Reforms: The Internationalization of Russian Agriculture* (New York: Palgrave Macmillan 2013).

with alcoholism after the shutting down of its factory, conveys the gravity of the situation in small towns far removed from the metropolises.[11]

Myshkin is in the Yaroslavl region of Central Russia, which is home to two large oil refineries.[12] A portion of Myshkin's population is employed at gas compression and oil pumping stations, but both enterprises provide only several hundred jobs and cannot satisfy the labour demand in this town of 6,000 inhabitants. Over its history, Myshkin has been classified as both a village and a small town by the national authorities, its status oscillating between both. Since regaining town status in 1991, Myshkin has faced the challenge of developing a viable development strategy in the absence of large production facilities.

Tourism is considered as a last resort by many Russian small towns desperate to build or restore large production facilities. Myshkin, however, did not seem to be in an especially favourable position to create a tourist industry. First, the town does not possess a rich or interesting history. Since its founding in the sixteenth century, it has been a small village or town, a home for local merchants. It has never been the site of any noteworthy historical events nor the birthplace of any celebrities. Second, Myshkin has few attractions apart from two cathedrals of limited architectural significance. Third, Myshkin is far from the major highways. It lies on the left bank of the Volga River, between Uglich and Rybinsk, the second largest industrial city in the Yaroslavl region. When the tourist industry in Myshkin was launched, river cruise vessels did not even stop at this small settlement.

These circumstances made it virtually impossible for Myshkin to capitalise on its history or architecture or use Uglich as its model, a neighbouring town dating from the early period of Russian statehood which witnessed many local wars between princes and the murder of the son of Ivan the Terrible.[13] In addition, Myshkin had never possessed a tourist industry on which it could rely to develop its self-presentation and infrastructure. Realising its lack of tourist allurement, this small town adopted a rather enterprising strategy of radical symbolic construction. Myshkin performed a risky branding, taking the mouse as its symbol

---

11 Daria Dimke and Irina Koryukhina. "Zavod po proizvodstvu vremeni." ["A Time-Production Factory."] *Otechestvennye Zapiski* 50, no. 5 (2012).

12 Yaroslavl region is 37th in Russia by GRP, as of 2013. http://www.gks.ru/bgd/regl/b15_14p /IssWWW.exe/Stg/d02/10-02.doc (accessed 15. 4. 2017).

13 Uglich has also been rather successful in developing tourism, with an annual tourist influx of 334,000 in 2012. However, by the early 1990s it already had a clear image, as well as a developed infrastructure and experience in tourism.

("mysh" means "mouse" in Russian). History was replaced by a set of mouse-centred narratives told to tourists. This plan meant integrating some pseudo-authentic elements into an established fairyland context and creating a dozen museums that exhibit seemingly everyday objects made interesting for tourists because of their immersion in the general structure of the phantasy. Thus, Myshkin constructed an operative symbolic matrix that could be used to generate new legends and museums. The distinctiveness of this strategy from the traditional history-oriented approach is immediately recognizable in the way tourist agencies advertise the town, inviting tourists to enter a "revived fairy-tale."[14]

The success of this ambitious project seems indisputable. In the mid-1990s, Myshkin had no tourist industry at all; by 2012, the annual number of tourists had skyrocketed to 165,000, according to statistics provided by the local administration. What accounted for this result? What role did the local community play in accomplishing this change? How has the transformation affected the community's life?

3. Authenticity and Phantasy

Tourist professionals often neglect an important consideration familiar to scholars in the field of tourist studies: the success of touristic enterprises does not depend on the number of objects objectively worth visiting but on the ability to produce a specific tourist experience. Many Russian small towns that witnessed the closure of important factories made considerable investments later in attempting to switch to the tourist industry. Although many reasonably believe that they have sufficient historically important monuments to interest tourists, few have actually succeeded in tourism. It may have been that they simply did not pay enough attention to producing a memorable tourist experience.[15]

What is the tourist experience, and how does it emerge? Although the answers suggested by scholars differ considerably, John Urry summarises the crucial features: the tourist experience emerges only when individuals break temporarily with everyday life and suspend ordinary, everyday

---

14 See, for instance a tour program called "Fairy-tales of a provincial town." http://www.pstour. ru/shkolnye-tury-po-zolotomu-kolcu/skazki-provincialnogo-goroda/ (accessed 15. 4. 2017).

15 What is meant by experience here is not simply a view or an impression, but a set of interrelated meanings organizing the subject's inner spiritual world. The concept goes back to the notion of lived experience (*Erlebnis*), suggested by the German philosopher Wilhelm Dilthey. See: Wilhelm Dilthey, *Gesammelte Schriften. Bd. VI* (Leipzig 1924), 313.

experience.[16] Tourists do not merely look for new information or even new experiences; they seek an opportunity to adopt a completely new vision of or attitude towards the world, although they realize that the suspension of their normal routine is only temporary.[17] In other words, for the tourist industry, it is essential to create situations that transform the attitude of tourists for some period of time.

Theories of the tourist experience emphasise various productive ways of modifying attitude. While some researchers claim that the proper experience can be gained only by restoring or simulating *authenticity*, others point out that some successful tourist projects achieve the required attitude by constructing *phantasy*. Both modes of generating the tourist experience involve a laborious processing of history, albeit in different ways. For small towns, history appears to be a reservoir for productive work. Sometimes, it requires effort to restore the atmosphere of authenticity by reconstructing the true history of a particular city, digging into its past to excavate famous persons or events related to it. In other cases, history must be amended to make the place worth seeing, and some pseudo-historical narratives that fit the general image of the place must be created. In still other cases, real history is completely replaced by a narrative that deliberately breaks all ties with reality, as happens in the construction of phantasy. However, we shall argue that these strategies of dealing with history elucidated by different theorists are not mutually exclusive and can in fact be combined to build a complex narrative featuring elements with varying historical veracity.

The significance of authenticity was brought to the forefront as early as 1973 by Dean MacCannell who argued that contemporary tourists are preoccupied with a search for authenticity. Contrary to Daniel Boorstin's earlier view that tourists are satisfied with glancing at the surface of objects and never want to go behind the stage,[18] MacCannell believes that nowadays tourists are constantly searching for authentic experience not designed purposefully for them – they always want to see the backstage, not the frontstage (these terms are borrowed from the work of sociologist

---

16 Urry, *The Tourist Gaze*.

17 Theories of tourist experience tend to rely extensively on phenomenological notions, such as "attitude" and "authenticity" (see below). The idea of "natural attitude," corresponding to ordinary everyday life and multiple ways to modify it, was suggested by Edmund Husserl in his *Ideas for a Pure Phenomenology and Phenomenological Philosophy: First Book*, Dordrecht 1998. For a further discussion of the use of phenomenological concepts in tourist studies see: Ning Wang, "Rethinking authenticity in tourism experience," *Annals of Tourism Research* 26, no. 2 (1999).

18 Daniel J. Boorstin, *The Image: A Guide to Pseudo-Events in America* (New York: Harper 1961).

Erving Goffman).[19] MacCannell adds that producers of the tourist experience are well aware of this desire and skillfully manipulate backstage experience, providing tourists with a kind of "staged authenticity."

MacCannell's paper precipitated a long tradition of studies on authenticity in tourism. The concept of authenticity itself has been revisited several times. Much attention has been paid to so-called "existential" authenticity (as opposed to the authenticity of particular objects) – that is, to the particular experience of authenticity that tourists seek.[20] Drawing on the philosophy of Martin Heidegger, Ning Wang demonstrates that the search for existential authenticity is driven by a profound feeling of inauthenticity of being, characteristic of Western modernity. Nostalgia and romanticism stimulate the hunt for authenticity; there is always a feeling that something has been lost, that some preordained harmony has been corrupted, and everyday life is forever marked by inauthenticity.[21] The search for the lost harmony presumes the original unity of man with nature and the human community. Nostalgic images portray man as undifferentiated from nature and community – all three merge into one another, protecting man and unburdening him from the anxiety of his individualistic being.

Some scholars have criticised the theory of authenticity, pointing out that, in a world filled with simulacra, authenticity can no longer be attained nor even truly sought, even in its staged form.[22] Indeed, the success of the Disneyland model in tourism attests at least to the fact that authenticity is not the sole way to change attitudes and create a consistent tourist experience. Another kind of modification occurs when "real-life" history is supplemented with, or supplanted by, myths and fairy tales to make an object or territory more attractive to visitors.[23] Although tourists can sometimes attribute a certain degree of reality to myths, these are generally understood to be merely phantasies.[24] Their effect arises from combining real-world elements (e.g., settings, surroundings, buildings)

---

19   MacCannell, "Staged authenticity: Arrangements of social space in tourist settings," 593.

20   Carol Steiner and Yvette Reisinger, "Understanding existential authenticity," *Annals of Tourism Research* 33, no. 2 (2006), 299–318.

21   Wang, "Rethinking authenticity in tourism experience," 358–359.

22   George Ritzer and Allan Liska, "McDisneyization and 'post-tourism:' Complementary perspectives on contemporary tourism." In *Touring Cultures: Transformations of Travel and Theory*, ed. Chris Rojek and John Urry (London and New York 2003), 107.

23   John Hannigan, *Fantasy City* (London 1998).

24   Husserl has suggested that in phantasy, as opposed to both ordinary life and hallucination, we can have a clear image of the objects and at the same time understand that they are unreal: Edmund Husserl, *Phantasy, Image Consciousness, and Memory* (Dordrecht 2005), 4.

with purely fantastic characters and events. When exploring a city, tourists often prefer to listen to fairy tales, occasionally intermeshed with 'real' history. In other words, producing a tourist experience in a city sometimes relies on generating exciting myths rather than on digging up the "real" past. Some tourist sites may even reject history entirely and become attractive by completely transporting tourists into fairy tales.

Although authenticity theories and the phantasy approach are usually presented as two opposing perspectives,[25] they are not necessarily incompatible. Tourists can appreciate authentic objects within phantasy. In fact, as we shall demonstrate, the fairy-tale narrative of Myshkin reinforces the experience of genuineness, endowing ordinary objects with an aura of authenticity.

4. Branding the Mouse

The development of the tourist industry in Myshkin was a conscious, strategic choice by local elites, including public officials, cultural activists and members of the administration (mostly newcomers from the late Soviet years). A dozen representatives from these groups created and promoted the ideology of tourism. The industry has been largely and is increasingly controlled by the local administration. Although a number of small entrepreneurs are involved, they are coordinated by the dominant city-owned enterprise that generates an ever-growing share of revenue.

When discussing the tourist project in Myshkin, local officials tend to emphasise the unfavourable initial conditions and the town's lack of a history that would attract tourists: "Myshkin is a self-made town. Uglich and the like are popular due to their great history, [...] whilst our Myshkin – well, there are churches, but [there's no] history as such." (Excerpt from an interview with a local official.)

Since the town was initially cut off from the main transport routes and almost inaccessible to tourists, the local administration faced the challenge of persuading tourist agencies to make cruise ships stop in Myshkin and send tour buses to the town. The task was especially difficult as Myshkin has no historically significant attractions that might draw tourist attention. Not surprisingly, tourist agencies were unwilling to risk including Myshkin in their itineraries.

---

25   See, for instance, Erich Cohen and Scott A. Cohen, "Current sociological theories and issues in tourism," *Annals of Tourism Research* 39, no. 4 (2012), 2177–2202.

Tourism advocates responded by suggesting a non-historical basis for manufacturing the tourist experience. Myshkin would make use of a legend about its foundation and the origin of its name. According to the myth, a prince hunting in the area became tired and fell asleep on the bank of the Volga River. Awakened by a mouse, he was angry with it at first but then realised that a snake had been approaching him, which meant that the mouse had saved his life. After escaping this danger, the prince ordered the construction of a temple in honour of Saints Boris and Gleb at the place of the incident. The town that grew up around the new building was named Myshkin. Multiple versions of this legend might differ in details, but they all emphasise the key role of a mouse as the prince's saviour.

In the mid-1990s, local activists seeking a brand solution attractive to tourists eventually drew on the legend. The mouse became the official iconic image for the town, the local coat of arms was altered to include a small mouse, and the authorities heavily promoted depictions of mice.

"And so I told them [acquaintances from another town], there's nothing to laugh about. It's all dead serious. We make money on mice." (Representative of tourism industry)

"So, little by little, this mouse entered each and every sphere." (Local official)

"It is as if Myshkin is identical to mouse." (Local activist)

Making the mouse the town symbol, opening the first Museum of the Mouse and holding a mouse-themed festival in 1996 paid off shortly, when tourist agencies agreed to change their travel schedule and some vessels introduced an additional stop at Myshkin on the way to Uglich. The new fairy-tale town quickly became popular among tourists, especially children. It made a productive contrast to other towns on the river-cruise routes that tended to capitalise on their historical heritage. Describing the attractiveness of Myshkin, tourists emphasise the town's inventiveness and ability to play up its features to an extent rarely matched at other sites on the cruise route.

However, as suggested by theories of phantasy, it is not enough simply to coin a symbol or a legend; the real work is to build an environment that suspends ordinary life and draws tourists into a new reality. Myshkin is not the only Russian town to adopt the constructivist strategy, although it was likely the first and stands as a role model. In 1997, Petushki, a town of 14,000 in the Vladimir region, followed Myshkin's example of capitalising on the animal contained in the town's name and opened

Fig. 3: Summer street in Myshkin. Photo by courtesy of Varvara Kobyshcha.

the Cock Museum. However, this museum draws only 2,500 visitors annually, compared to the 65,000 at the Mouse Museum in Myshkin. This difference can be largely explained by the context: the Cock Museum is positioned as an art institution and emphasises the aesthetic value of the objects exhibited, whereas the Mouse Museum invites visitors "into the Mouse kingdom-state," downplaying the aesthetic qualities of the items on display.

To create a full-scale phantasy world, the whole town of Myshkin has been redesigned thematically. The city centre features the Mouse Museum and the Palace of the Mouse Queen, and the town itself is often referred to as Mouseland. As described by Myshkin's English-language website: "The town is full with tales and legends. The very atmosphere and architecture of the town take us as though to a completely different world, to another planet – the planet ruled by Mice. [...] Thousands of tourists from all over the world visit the small mouse town every year to kneel before the great Mice."[26]

This manner of manufacturing the tourist experience builds on a narrative that is not only indifferent to the town's "real" history but is even

---

26   http://eng.mouseland.ru/mushkin.html (accessed 16. 7. 2014). The website no longer exists.

conspicuously a-historical. However, this has proven to be quite con-
structive in Myshkin precisely because it can produce a whole fantastic
microcosm that suspends ordinary attitude and replaces it with a stream
of phantasy that remains almost uninterrupted as long as tourists stay in
Myshkin. Securing the continuation of the experience is among the key
tasks of local tourist industry operators. Visitors to Myshkin tend to fall
into three broad categories by mode of travel: individual travellers and
groups arriving by either ship or bus. The two latter categories, which
account for more than 90% of the tourist flow,[27] are immediately met at
their point of arrival by local guides responsible for conducting visitors
along carefully developed routes, bringing them from one museum to
another and insulating them from anything that could interrupt the
impression of being in a fairy tale. This strategy perfectly matches the
disposition of the tourists, who tend to complain that, without constant
guidance, they feel as if they are "blind."

5. Local History: A Movement beneath the Business

Constructivist theories emphasising the phantasy element of the tourist
experience cannot fully account for the tourism success in Myshkin. A
constructivist approach to history is especially strong in producing the
experience of phantasy, but it has to rely on other types of historical
work to mobilise local inhabitants to participate in the collective action
of manufacturing the image presented to tourists. The case of Myshkin
demonstrates that the simultaneous operation of different modes of dealing with history creates a stable and profitable image. Moreover, despite
all the differences, these modes can intermingle, reinforce one another
and create opportunities for the production of new staged authenticities.

Until the mid-1990s, when the mouse became the town's brand and
supplanted the historical narrative, a group of local historians in Myshkin
worked on maintaining a collective memory. The group was organised in
the 1970s by an enthusiast and resembled an association of Boy Scouts,

---

27 The levee is more important and accounts probably for three quarters of the flow. More ac-
curate estimates are difficult to make because official statistics only count the tourists coming
through agencies. Agencies deliver tourists to Myshkin mostly by river; a large portion of
them are state employees from Moscow and St. Petersburg who get tickets for the cruise from
their trade unions at a reduced price. Since the unions have a long-term contract with tourist
agencies, many tourists are offered the cruise on the Volga River several times, so that they
come to Myshkin more than once. Several respondents told us that this was their fifth trip to
the town.

consisting mainly of schoolchildren who sought and collected artefacts from earlier times throughout the town. Anything that looked old and had a flavour of authenticity was collected in the first museum of local history.

In the 1960s, local history (*kraevedenie*, knowledge of the region) flourished in the Soviet Union as a tool for reshaping patriotism. It has an ambiguous relationship with historical science, being rather the practice of collecting items of material culture and writing biographies of local celebrities than a scientific undertaking. Local history emerged in the years of the Russian Empire and, after thirty years of oblivion under dictator Josef Stalin, was revitalised to make "exhibitions of the regional past and its material culture [...] affirm contemporary values of collective leadership, democracy, and the construction of socialism."[28] According to the new conception of local history, the values espoused by the dominant ideology of the Communist Party were too abstract to create love for the motherland, but knowledge of local history could effectively create attachment to the land. The efforts by local historians survived the collapse of communist ideology and continue to instil local patriotism in the absence of a state-imposed framework.

As part of the general *kraevedenie* movement,[29] local historians in Myshkin promoted local patriotism. One of their objectives was the preservation of town status, since Myshkin had been officially reclassified as a village several times. At some point, the group acquired enough symbolic power to persuade the authorities and the population that fighting for town status was important. As adults, the former schoolchildren took up positions in the library, museum and other institutions that contributed to communication between local historians from Myshkin and other towns. Myshkin became one of the key centres of local history in the Yaroslavl region, but most importantly, local historians gradually developed into an organised community claiming a monopoly on the symbolic representation of the town.

When a journalist from Moscow suggested the idea of making the mouse the town's brand, local historians were the key group authorising this decision. Despite the inconsistency between the symbolism of the

---

28 Victoria Donovan, "'Going backwards, we stride forwards': Kraevedenie museums and the making of local memory in North West Russia, 1956–1981," *Forum for Anthropology and Culture* 7 (2012), 215.

29 As is the case in many other Russian small towns, local historians in Myshkin are proud to have been in communication with the famous philologist Dmitry Likhachev, who is usually credited with being the founder of *kraevedenie*.

fictitious mouse and the hunt for authentic local history, it was generally believed that rebranding could make Myshkin better known and contribute to economic and cultural development. The museum of local history was redesigned and officially renamed The National Museum – Mouse Museum, and local historians started playing important roles in the tourist project. They drew attention to Myshkin by arranging events, communicating with colleagues in other regions and spreading the word about the new brand.

Even more importantly, a link was established between schoolchildren and the tourist industry. Local history was incorporated into the curriculum in secondary schools in Myshkin at the same time that schoolteachers became involved in the tourist business. Most tourist enterprises (e.g., museums, guided tours, production of handmade mouse figurines) involve local historians, so children are quickly socialised in the industry. Some work in the summer as vendors of handmade products, while others are trained as tour guides. Some even try making museums of their own, following the established pattern.

> "A current director of the tourist enterprise had previously worked at the school. At that period, children were taken on the guided tours all the time. [...] I had a museum of my own. It used to be quite famous. My friends and I, we collected old things in courtyards and established a museum in my grandfather's garage. We collected matchboxes. We collected old things from grandmothers. We did not work for anybody. We charged money for visits." (Recent graduate of local secondary school)

The synthesis of phantasy and local history opens up opportunities for yet another type of tourist experience. However successful the symbol of the mouse might be, tourists confess that they inevitably tire of it. A challenge for the industry emerging here is to diversify the exhibits without breaking the narrative of Mouseland.

The carefully preserved atmosphere of the fairy tale creates an aura which can transform ordinary objects into valuable cultural units. Once a fantastic experience is produced, it can convey additional meaning even to exhibits not related to the mouse symbol. Consequently, some objects generally seen in local history museums acquire additional importance; an old salt-cellar or an axe exhibited in the National Museum of Myshkin is perceived differently by tourists already floating in a world of phantasy. Matchboxes, Soviet-era tins and other small items are easily turned into museum objects by relating them to the mouse theme. To endow ordinary material things with considerable symbolic significance, it is sufficient to declare that the objects were collected by "mouskins" who "took them into their burrow" (that is, by children who brought them to the museum), as museum guides put it.

Such exhibits provide a viable response to the tourist hunger for authenticity. The objects establish a quasi-historical connection between the exhibitions and the town. In these settings, objects acquire a flavour of authenticity and appear to represent tradition. Through combining phantasy and authenticity, Myshkin addresses two different demands by tourists: for fairy tales and for tradition.

Moreover, the aura that assigns importance to ordinary objects creates opportunities to make authentic what is in reality completely artificial. In addition to old objects exhibited in museums in Myshkin, there is yet another type of appeal, which might be called a pseudo-authentic tourist attraction. A range of museums specialise in presenting pseudo-traditional practices, crafts and artefacts. For instance, at the Flax Museum, the House of Crafts and the Valenok Museum, tourists look at traditional methods of producing certain household items. However, these so-called "traditional crafts" are rather late inventions; they have no long-standing history in Myshkin and were devised for the sake of drawing visitors. In addition, as a reminder of the town's symbol, numerous mice appear in a fairy-tale manner in even the most authentic activities, tourist attractions and museums (e.g., toys made of flax, *valenki* – felt boots – with mouse ears, and the like).

The nearby village of Martynovo is also part of the Myshkin tourist industry. It is presented as the homeland of a small, disappearing ethnic group (*katskari*) with its own language. Although there is no evidence that such a group ever existed, and the language is limited to several words, tours of the village are quite popular among travellers looking for authentic life and evanescent tradition. The institutions of the pseudo-authentic experience participate in the rearing of members of the host community and play a significant role in promoting the town itself.

6. Don't Spoil the Impression: The Ambiguous Status of the Local Community

Manufacturing the tourist experience, especially in the modes of radical phantasy construction and staged authenticity, often poses challenges to the sustainable development of local communities. Although tour-

Fig. 4: Locals of different ages gather at the entrance to a shop near the tourist route. Photo by courtesy of Varvara Kobyshcha.

ism might be salvific for the town's economy, it also complicates local identity and makes citizens worry about their place in a tourist-oriented town. As demonstrated, local historians in Myshkin could integrate the preservation of historical identity into the broader phantasy narrative. However, in addition to the issue of identity, there is a need to secure cooperation from local inhabitants. Doing so requires finding the right balance between involving citizens in the industry and, at the same time, protecting it from them.

The industry has had some clear, positive effects on the lives of citizens, creating jobs in both small businesses and the large city-owned tourist enterprise, and modernising the infrastructure. For instance, foodstuffs were long supplied to the local population through small shops owned by local businessmen. In 2014, however, two supermarkets were opened, leading to lower prices. On the other hand, the constant presence of tourists in the town also has negative effects: prices tend to be set for visitors from Moscow and St. Petersburg, who are much wealthier than the local population. Perhaps more importantly, a growing sentiment among citizens holds that the town has been turned into a "town for tourists, not for us," as many informants put it. Although the administration tends to emphasise the industry's contribution to the town's economic profitability, tourism is sometimes considered a necessary evil rather than a blessing. The integration of the local community has become important to prevent the increase of hostility towards tourists.

Tourism in Myshkin has flourished by building a fairy-tale world relatively isolated from the ordinary life of both tourists and hosts. The biggest town map which tourists encounter is called "The Kingdom of the Mouse" and painted in fairy-tale style on a wall inside the Mouse Palace (where Mouse King and Mouse Queen sit on their thrones). In the middle of the map is an enormous picture of the Mouse Palace, while other tourist attractions, including two cathedrals, look relatively small.

However, completely excluding locals from this staged phantasy of a mouse-centred town would be impossible. The preservation of the borders of the fairy tale requires some collaboration or at least consent from the town's inhabitants. To keep the experience of phantasy intact, the authorities need to protect it from various possible external

Fig. 5: Scene from a show for tourists in the Mouse Palace: the Mouse Queen talking to visitors. Photo by courtesy of Varvara Kobyshcha.

intrusions. Local townspeople can significantly influence the tourists' overall impression. Areas with sightseeing attractions need to be kept clean, and visitors expect the houses which appear on their path to be presentable and follow a unified style. Officials and activists understand that citizens could spoil the work of producing the right impression on tourists. Enlisting locals as allies is necessary to prevent the destruction of the front-stage.

"Tourists should be in good spirits from the very moment the ship arrives. And Heaven save us from leaving an unpleasant impression on tourists. [...] What could spoil the impression? Well, if one meets a drunken person in the street. A long time ago, we instructed our people, so things of that kind don't happen anymore. We have even succeeded in civilising city dwellers. And it's good that we have a newspaper where such matters are discussed. People in Myshkin are active themselves. [...] There is a real pride for their town and also a struggle for cleanliness, for beauty." (One of the founders of the local tourist industry).

Fig. 6: A warning sign in the town centre. The left side reads: "Smokers! Your cigarette butts are most unwelcome here. There is a trashcan near the museum." The front reads: "Please do not leave any garbage here. There is a trashcan near the museum." Photo by courtesy of Varvara Kobyshcha.

Several mechanisms promote collaboration among locals. Special prizes are granted for cleanliness and beauty, while well-known figures impose moral sanctions on those who spoil the view by redesigning the facade of their own homes. While arranging awards for best practices is a relatively simple undertaking, inducing self-restraint is a complicated task. In Myshkin, local officials hope to overcome this difficulty through the construction of a strong local community. Community-building takes place by means of patriotism and history lessons, which are viewed as interconnected. Such objects and activities as museums, lessons on local history and the victory memorial to Myshkin soldiers who fought in World War II are necessary for the successful schooling of members of the host community. The importance of education is constantly underlined:

A: "Local history lessons start in kindergarten. They are not part of the curriculum at this level, but local historians and teachers set up events for schoolchildren, arrange annual competitions and so on, everything about local history. They also set up museums at schools."
Q: "Is that really important?"
A: "It is very important. [...] This is the inculcation of love for the homeland."
(One of the founders of the local tourist industry.)

However, not everything in the town is meant to be presented to tourists, so there is also a need to protect the backstage from the gaze of tourists. In Myshkin, the border between the front- and the backstage is geographically visible as the tourist area is in the town centre near the embankment. All the museums are concentrated there, and all the tourist routes are designed to give visitors no incentive to leave the central area. Most tourists arrive on river cruises, so they are immediately picked up by guides upon disembarkation and controlled throughout the duration of their stay in Myshkin, usually 2–4 hours.

Guides and routes are especially important for creating and preserving the desired impression, so considerable effort is put into training programmes. The guides are taught to protect the backstage by channelling visitors along the set routes. They are also adept at satisfying those hungry for authenticity or simply eager to learn more about the town or who seek to look behind the staged fairy tale. Tour guides have special instructions prescribing which information to disclose. In interviews, tourists attest that local guides tend to present a positive image of the town, in sharp contrast to guides at many other tourist sites who often

Fig. 7: Display in the Mouse Palace featuring mice in various forms and sizes. Photo by courtesy of Varvara Kobyshcha.

complain about prevailing living conditions. Most importantly, the origin of the tour guides is of paramount consideration in the selection process, and only those from Myshkin itself are hired. It is assumed that they are more loyal to the town and its officials and more willing to present the setting in a favourable way.[30]

7. Conclusion

In the global economy, tourism is a viable alternative for many small towns, but developing this industry requires careful interplay with a town's history. The case of Myshkin demonstrates that there are multiple

---

30   The way the system works can be illustrated by the example of the maternity hospital closure, which took place in early 2013. Interviews with the local inhabitants reveal that a protest took place following the closure, and 1,000 people signed a petition against it. Informants usually highlighted the fact that a pregnant woman died soon afterwards due to the lack of medical care. Some tourists visiting the following summer were aware of the incident and asked the tour guides for details. The guides, however, tried to downplay the story since it might create an unpleasant impression of the town. They presented mutually contradictory versions of what

Fig. 8: A cruise ship on the Volga River near Myshkin. Photo by courtesy of Varvara Kobyshcha.

facets involved, and a successful tourist industry requires a combination of these. The tourist experience can be produced and heightened by suspending everyday life and immersing visitors within historical or pseudo-historical narratives. Although artificially constructed, myths can sometimes be a powerful means for generating the phantasy experience, but the local community always needs an identity for concerted, collective action, which is indispensable for maintaining the presentation of the city both on the front- and the backstage. Tourists tend to search for authenticity, and historical tradition is of crucial importance here since history justifies and underscores the claims put forward. As Eric Hobsbawm and Terence Ranger point out, the skilful invention of tradition is always employed to substantiate claims about the primordial unity of the community.[31]

However fictional the myths produced by the host town might be, there is always a place for the community behind the myth, a collective

happened, but always tended to conceal the unpleasant event itself, either by denying closure or claiming that it was proposed by the locals themselves or they simply evaded the question.

31 Eric J. Hobsbawm and Terence Ranger, *The Invention of Tradition* (Cambridge: Cambridge University Press 1992).

narrator who relates the myth to the tourist. Myth alone is never sufficient to manufacture an appropriate tourist experience – it must be accompanied by recourse to history and tradition, and be mediated by the presence of a community. The success of a tourist enterprise depends on integrating the politics of building a community with the practice of tourist management. The effectiveness of this work is crucial for the survival of small towns as both economic units and political unities.

Urban Cores and Urban Identity: Appropriating and Rejecting a City's History. The Case of Rethymno

Olga Moatsou

1. Small Towns in Greece

The city of Athens enjoys considerable attention from academics and researchers thanks to its long past, its history, as well as the unique urbanization processes it has experienced on many occasions since it became Greece's capital. Often, Greek cities are categorized into large metropoles (which include for instance Athens and Thessaloniki) and big cities (Larissa, Patra, Heraklion and Volos), and small towns.[1] And while there is an extended bibliography on Athens and Thessaloniki, and significant references regarding the various big cities, little can be found – particularly in non-Greek publications – on the small Greek towns. This present essay is an effort to shed some light on the life and urban identity in small towns in Greece and to shift the focus towards the way they changed in post-war and contemporary times.

1.1 Athens and Patterns of Expansion

During the post-war years the Greek countryside was devastated; by 1948, over 5,000 villages had been ruined.[2] What was worse, World War II was followed by a shattering civil war (1946–1949), forcing Greece to enter the 1950s in a state of penury. The reconstruction pro-gramme, mainly financed by foreign help, finally took place after 1949 and brought about urbanization and demographic changes. At the same time, reconstruction faced the problems of an overwhelmed Greek state,

---

1 For more analytical information, see Guy Burgel and Zakharias Demathas, *La Grèce face au troisième millénaire: Territoire, économie, société. 40 ans de mutations* (Athens: Panteion University of Social and Political Sciences 2001).

2 Thomas W. Gallant, *Modern Greece* (London: Arnold 2001).

and this, in turn, led to shortcomings in the legal framework, with much arbitrariness occurring due to both the lack of institutions and of efficient monitoring. Urban growth eventually exploded in Athens and a limited number of the larger cities, leading them to monopolize the interest of the government, which made intense efforts to improve life and introduce modernity. In the provinces, however, reconstruction remained dormant and led to the creation of a sharp distinction between the significant, large urban centres and the backward, often still rural small towns.

The chasm between the expanding Greek cities and the destitute provinces deepened in the course of the 1950s, producing a specific pattern of expansion.[3] Athens dominated political and scientific debate and was an inevitable pole of attraction for research and planning.[4] It received significant funds for its growth and attracted investments and migration. The imbalance between the capital and the small towns was intensified by the fact that the Greek government had become highly centralized, with decision-making, fund management and authority being located in Athens.

A defining element in the growth of contemporary Athens was the construction delirium that started in the mid-1950s. Following a long period of poverty and urban decay, in order to rejuvenate the economy and to replenish the missing housing stock, the Greek government encouraged the building sector and thus caused a boom in the industry. This was most evident in the frenetic construction of a unique structure called the "polykatoikia,"[5] which became the most widespread housing form in contemporary Greece. Such apartment blocks replaced build-

---

3   It has been postulated that this pattern of centralization can be observed in more southern European countries. See Martin Baumeister, "Die Hydra der Moderne. Masseneinwanderung und Wohnungspolitik in Madrid unter der Franco-Diktatur." In *Informationen zur modernen Stadtgeschichte – Städte in Südeuropa* 1 (2009), Berlin: Deutsches Institut für Urbanistik 2009, 47–59.

4   See more in Olga Moatsou, *Polykatoikia, 1960–2000: Entrepreneurial Housing, from Athens to Rethymno*, (Lausanne: École polytechnique fédérale de Lausanne (EPFL) 2014), Chapter 3.1.

5   The term refers to a multi-storey building of apartments operating under the condominium system and translates into "multi-residence." The post-war polykatoikia was interwoven with private initiative and remains in collective memory as equivalent to shameless speculation practiced by uneducated individuals. See also: Ioanna Theocharopoulou, *Urbanization and the emergence of the polykatoikia: Habitat and identity*, Athens 1830–1974, New York: Columbia University 2007; O. Moatsou, Polykatoikia, 1960–2000, Lausanne 2014; Yannis Aesopos, "Die 'Polykatoikia' als Modul der modernen Stadt. Entwicklung des Appartamentenhauses in Athen," *Bauwelt* 29 (2004), 14–21; Nikos Kalogeras, "I astiki polykatoikia kai i synecheia tou modernismou stin Ellada" [The Urban Polykatoikia and the Resumption of Modernism in Greece], *Design + Art in Greece* 29 (1998), 36–46.

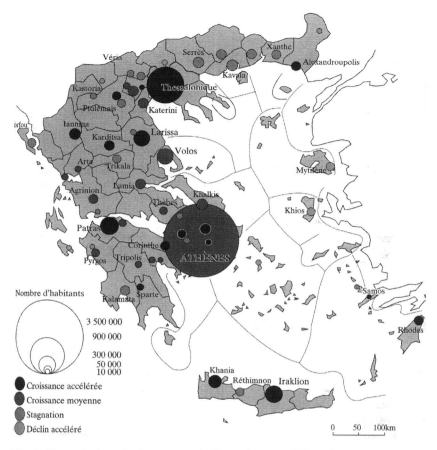

Fig. 1: The evolution of urban centres in Greece between 1961 and 1991, showing Athens as the indisputable centre.
Source: Guy Burgel, Zakharias Demathas. *La Grèce face au troisième millénaire: territoire, économie, société. 40 ans de mutations.* Athens: Panteion University of Social and Political Sciences, 2001, 45.

ings in the old city, whose former neoclassical cityscape has since been nostalgically praised.[6]

---

6   The reason for the collective emotional recollection of the lost past in contemporary Greek society can be traced back to the raising of buildings, notably the polykatoikias, during the construction boom of the 1950s. In short, the entrepreneurs behind the polykatoikias relied on a unique legal and economic framework, known as the antiparohi, as well as the prevalence of condominium ownership, which did not require having sufficient funds or expertise in order to erect a building. More can be found in: Moatsou, *Polykatoikia, 1960–2000*, 165.

2. Tale of a Town

In order to place the focus on the small towns of Europe, a closer look into the development and identity perceptions of a Greek town is hereby offered; the example taken is the town of Rethymno on the island of Crete. Once part of the Venetian *Regno di Candia* and subsequently of the Ottoman Empire, contemporary Rethymno is an amalgam of several identities. First of all, the inhabitants embrace their local traditions; at the same time, they consider their city to have a unique European inheritance due to the presence of Venetian elements. Furthermore, they accept foreign influences, as the remains of the Ottoman period testify. Moreover, Rethymno is nowadays a popular tourist destination. Consequently, its actual domestic fabric exhibits a rudimentarily modern cityscape extending around the initial settlement, the Venetian and Ottoman core called Old Town, which was listed in the 1970s.[7]

As already mentioned, while Athens and a few other large cities went through significant growth in the post-war era, the Greek provinces, and thus Rethymno, remained abandoned and impoverished until well into the 1960s. A closer look at its history and into the creation of historical layers in its urban tissue is hereby offered.

2.1 A Long History in Brief

The island of Crete passed from the Byzantine Empire into the control of the Republic of Venice in 1204 when Constantinople was taken over by the crusaders of the Fourth Crusade. During the years of the so-called *Regno di Candia* that lasted until 1669, a number of Venetian nobles took up residence in the city in order to monitor trade and to control the Cretan population. In the early 14th century, the island was divided into four prefectures and the town of Rethymno became the capital of its homonymous prefecture, as well as the seat of the island's governor. A prosperous phase of Venetian rule was marked by the arrival of Venetian architect Michele Sanmicheli in 1538 and the erection of a large number of residences, churches, shops and fortifications,[8] and the introduction

---

7   This part of the town will be referred to as Old Town, with the capital letters indicating that historic settlements in the centre of southern European cities are a unique characteristic; also, in the Greek vernacular, it is recognizable as a reference to the old part of a town. In contrast, modern districts are simply referred to as the new town.

8   Overall, Rethymno presents perhaps the largest preserved Venetian residential area built in the Renaissance to be found outside of Italy, Michael Herzfeld, *A Place in History: Social and Monumental Time in a Cretan Town* (Princeton, N.J.: Princeton University Press 1991).

of basic city planning which gave shape to what was previously a mere settlement.

In 1646, Ottoman troops took over the town of Rethymno. Overall during their stay in Crete, the Ottomans brought about very limited changes to the urban structure of cities and building stock, mainly adapting the existing edifices and residences to their needs. Their presence lasted until the late-19th century, specifically 1898, the year that the Cretan State was founded. In 1912, the island of Crete finally became part of Greece. Until that time, the population of Rethymno had remained within the fortifications built in the 16th century. It was only after the arrival of immigrants from Asia Minor between 1922 and 1924 that the city extended beyond the Venetian wall.

This significant migratory phenomenon occurred following the Treaty of Lausanne in 1923,[9] when a large number of refugees were deported from Asia Minor by the Turkish state, in exchange for the Muslim population living in Greece. The Muslim inhabitants of Crete who had to leave and settle in Turkey were known as "Tourkokritikoi," or "Turkish-Cretans," a broad umbrella term for people with various relationships to Turkey. The "Tourkokritikoi" were often people who had Greek ancestry but had converted to Islam or married into families of Turkish origin. They could also be Cretans whose ancestors had come to Crete during the Ottoman occupation and thus had what was considered to be a Turkish background.

The "Tourkokritikoi" were well-integrated members of the local society before the Greco-Turkish War.[10] The demographic shock that came with the population exchange affected Rethymno's residential neighbourhoods greatly. Some of those arriving from the opposite coast of the Aegean Sea found Rethymno inferior to their hometowns and its economic potential insufficient. They refused to settle down and moved instead to other areas of the country.[11] The refugees who remained were given the homes of the Turkish-Cretans who had departed, in compen-

---

9 For Greece, the Treaty of Lausanne marked the conclusion of the Greco-Turkish War in 1919–1922.

10 Approximately 4,000 Turkish-Cretans were affected by this treaty and were forced to abandon their homes in Crete for a new life in Turkey. By the same token, another 4,200 people living in Turkey arrived in Rethymno. For more insight into the "Tourkokritikoi" see: Yorgos Fryganakis, *I Rethemniotiki pena kai oi prosfyges tis Mikrasiatikis katastrofis* [The Rethemniot Pen and the Refugees of the Asia Minor Catastrophe] (Rethymno: Rethemnos newspaper 2011).

11 During the first thirty years of the 20th century, the city's population dropped by three thousand. Census 1928, see Herzfeld, *A Place in History*.

sation for their own lost properties. However, some of these homes were unavailable because they were often taken over by Rethemniots who did not want to allow the newcomers to reside close to them, thus forcing them to build their own quarters directly outside of the city, in an unauthorized manner that was tolerated by the authorities.[12]

With respect to urban planning, a street plan as well as construction regulations were introduced for the first time in 1930 with two decrees, which set the boundaries of the Old Town, naming specific streets as its limits.[13] At the time, Rethymno consisted of the "official," administrative centre situated within the fortifications and the surrounding settlements, "carrying racial [...] or professional characteristics."[14] This segregation, which deserves closer anthropological analysis, was based on the logic of religious identity, or of mother tongue, and not on the question of actual race. For example, among those settlements had been the lepers' neighbourhood and those of people originating from other areas of Greece, particularly of people whose ancestry had led back to Turkey and were Muslim. Inter-war Rethymno consisted of the Old Town, whose streets were greatly widened, and the New Town surrounding it.

2.2 The 1950's: An Invisible Economic Boom

During the Second World War, many of the Old Town's monuments suffered damage or were entirely destroyed. The only reconstruction project was the erection of a few homes known as *vomvoplikta*, meaning bombed-out, in reference to the German bombings. The government only issued a compulsory master plan with a Royal Decree in 1948,[15] modifying the pre-existing decree of 1930 and securing the fortress as a protected site. With this decree, building laws were set for plots, but the city structure described was much looser than that for Athens. Nevertheless, an indis-

---

12   In other words, refugees were forced to squat in the outskirts of the city. These makeshift homes were accepted by the local authorities, who knew that they were unable to provide state-built settlements. Also, they failed to convince those individuals who took over the homes which the people who went to Turkey left behind to hand them over to the refugees. They therefore turned a blind eye to the refugees' self-made, unauthorized homes. Fryganakis, *I Rethemniotiki pena*.

13   The decrees were a Royal Decree issued on 4 July 1930 in the Government Gazette number 228A, and a Presidential Decree of 5 July 1930, published in the Government Gazette 229A.

14   Michalis Deligiannakis, *Nomos Rethymnou, chorikes paremvaseis, nomothesia* [Municipality of Rethymno, Spatial Interventions, Regulations] (Rethymno: Kalaitzakis 2005), 26. Translated by the author.

15   Royal Decree of 9 March 1948, Government Gazette 62.

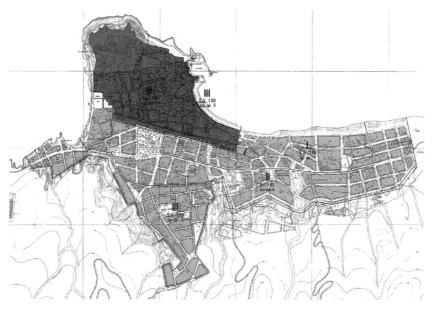

Fig. 2: Rethymno's plan in 1978; the pale grey part shows the new town, and the dark contains the Old Town.
Source: Visualization created by the author based on the official map exposing Rethymno's building zones from 1978, retrieved from the City's Authorities in 2011.

putably dense urban structure was the goal, since the enforced building system was contiguous (meaning that sides of buildings had to be joined) and plot occupation ratios were also high. The actual height of the buildings, on the other hand, was set lower than that in the capital city.

This happened, however, during the years 1945–1949 when Greece was suffering the ravages of a bloody civil war and the large-scale reconstruction programme in 1949–1952 allocated little space for putting the right infrastructure in place and issuing enough city master plans. The existing master plans, such as the one for Rethymno mentioned earlier, could never be integrally implemented. It was only in 1953, a year considered a milestone for the Greek economy as it marked the beginning of systematic development,[16] that the foundations for the enhancement of transportation, electricity, telecommunications and the financial sec-

---

16   I. E. Mavromatis, *Oikonomia tis Kritis 1951–1981*. Vol. A. [The Economy of Crete 1951–1981], Heraklio, 1989.

tor were set.[17] Nonetheless, the resulting bloom was noticeable only in Athens, Thessaloniki, and some of the other large cities. In 1957, Swiss journalist Manuel Gasser visited Crete as a reporter for *Weltwoche* and sojourned for three weeks. This trip, he wrote, was a favoured one among art-loving travellers. Comparing his destination to the Cyclades, he declared that Crete lacked the landmarks and the picturesque landscapes of Syros, Mykonos, Naxos or Santorini. "Crete, he wrote, is the haphazard accumulation of houses, huts and stables. [...] Crete exited the Middle Ages without going through a transitional period, straight into Bakelite and the common Nylon."[18] While the rest of Greece was already on its way to an economic miracle, the prospect of Crete and Rethymno, which had yet to receive attention, funds and integral planning, sharing in the boom remained distant.

2.3 The 1960s and 1970s: Planning a Town Outside of a Town

In the years that followed, Rethymno remained a poor town suffering from urban degradation. Its resources were agriculture, as well as the olive oil soap industry, present on the island since at least Ottoman times thanks to the abundance of olive trees. However, such major commercial activities where gradually set aside after the arrival of tourism and building speculation in Rethymno in the late-1960s. At the same time, a population increase was observed for the first time since the war, with the return of economic migrants from Athens and from Germany.

During the 1960s, the call for a comprehensive rejuvenation programme that would promote social development and treat the city as a living organism emerged in planners' discussions on a national scale. This change was traceable to the first issue of the architectural magazine *Architecture in Greece* (*Architektonika Themata*), in which noted architects debated the focal points of urban planning, the hypertrophy of Athens, and the importance of heritage. More specifically, in reference to Crete,

---

17 Apart from 1953 being often referred to as the end of the post-war era in Europe, i.e. Tony Judt, *Postwar: A History of Europe Since 1945* (London: Heinemann 2005), it was also the year that the Greek drachma was devalued in order to become more competitive. Indeed, this measure helped restrain inflation and encouraged imports, thus marking the start of the boom for the Greek economy. Not least, the European Recovery Program (Marshall Plan) was completed at that time.

18 Found in: Ioannis Kalitsounakis, "Entyposeis Elvetou periigitou apo tin Kriti" [Impressions of Crete by a Swiss Traveller] *Kritiki Protochronia*, no. 3 (1963), 12–18. For the original text see Manuel Grasser, "Wanderungen auf Kreta, Feriennotizen von M. G.," *Weltwoche*, no. 1227, (17 Mai 1957). Translated by the author.

urban planner Thales Argyropoulos noted that the perspectives of small Greek towns had grown because they had "escaped the frustration of the village." They were still "in touch with nature and primary production" and had a "potential for modest industrial development."[19]

In Rethymno, planning efforts were resumed in 1965, when surrounding settlements were integrated into the city plan. However, the results were often different than in the initial plan. To give an example, the once peripheral neighbourhood of Mastabas[20] was meant to become a garden city (marked with the number III on the previous map). Unfortunately, subsequent modifications, building coefficient augmentations and land fragmentation undermined the initial goals. Thus, contemporary Mastabas merged into Rethymno city with only slightly lower building requirements. With regard to tourism, although the military dictatorship had succeeded in encouraging the construction of hotels of an excessively large scale in other areas of the country, Rethymno's accommodation facilities remained modest. Until well into the 1960s, most hotels were merely inns or hostels, providing for the essential needs of the few travellers to the town, and were situated in the city centre.

In their "Master Plan and Tourist Development of Rethymno,"[21] a group of architects, civil and electrical engineers, economists, and lawyers foresaw a ribbon development along the seafront with the addendum that such a pattern would be suitable for a small coastal town. They also proposed a "conscious centre," the separation of services and the organization of "neighbourhood units" as key aspects. However, with the *coup d'état* occurring after the publication of this Master Plan, its realization was halted. Later on, in the spirit of preservation consciousness, the building laws for the old town of Rethymno were revised in 1967 and it was classified as a historic settlement, thus becoming a solid core.[22] It is interesting to consider that this decision was only reached after a *fait accompli*, the erection of a disproportionally large and high *polykatoikia* on the borderline of the Old Town which forced the authorities to push

---

19 Thales Argyropoulos, "I poleodomia kai i elliniki polis" [Town Planning and the Greek Town], *Architektonika Themata* 1 (1967), 41.

20 The name probably originates from the Arabic word for an Egyptian tomb; another area called Mastabas lies outside of Heraklion. Interestingly, they are both at a slightly higher altitude than the city centres.

21 D. Koutsoudakis and P. Arvanitakis, "Rythmistiki meleti Rethymnis kai touristikis anaptykseos ton akton tis" [Master Plan and Tourist Development of Rethymno], *Architektonika Themata* 2 (1968), 44–47.

22 Ministerial Decision 24946, 29 August 1967, *Government Gazette* of 30 October 1967, No. 606B.

for a strict delimitation of the historic settlement. Since nothing could be altered within the Old Town, in light of the lack of urban land available, Rethymno's linear expansion was also introduced in 1967.

The same principle was followed in the 1970s, when it was permitted to construct on peripheral plots, provided they were situated on a main street. The city spread not only along the seafront, but also on the main axes towards the mainland, thus embodying neighbouring settlements in its amorphous sprawl. Also, after the distribution of loans by the state for the preservation of traditional buildings in 1977,[23] Rethymno's Old Town was declared a traditional settlement in 1978 and detailed building laws were enacted.

In spite of those efforts, by the close of the 1970s, a large number of Rethymno inhabitants still lived in unhygienic dwellings, while tourism only started to grow at the end of the decade. It was during this time, too, that the University of Crete opened a department in Rethymno, creating a new population transfer thanks to the arrival of students. The university and tourism became fresh sources of income and urban transformation during the decade that followed.

2.4 From the 1980s to the Present

Until the 1980s, only sporadic statutes regulated Rethymno's outer-urban regions, since a complete development plan was not available. In 1985, construction outside of the city plan was made possible for large plots that were situated on a central street. Sadly, the law did not make clear distinctions between suburbia, the seafront, tourist areas or sites "of architectural interest," thus treating Rethymno's periphery as a non-differentiated whole and encouraging urban expansion. Then in 1986, a final urban extension plan was approved by construction authorities, changing the limits of the Old Town and increasing the building coefficient, plot coverage, and the number of floors allowed to three, thus bringing it closer to the structure of the outer, contemporary part.

Eventually, Rethymno's growth took place in a linear manner, which was, in any case, prescribed by geographical limits. The seafront on the north and also the hilly south prevented endless expansion, forcing Rethymno's urban fabric into a ribbon development on the major circulation axes as well as along the seafront, thus forming a unified area together with neighbouring settlements.

---

23 *Kritiki Epitheorisi* (17 July 1977).

The radical change that occurred, however, was the above-mentioned growth in tourism. With the number of air passengers increasing thirty-fold since the emergence of tourism on the island, and with travel within Crete itself becoming much more comfortable by the mid-1980s, it was only a matter of time before large hotel complexes were erected on the beachfront of Rethymno. Signs indicating "rooms to let" appeared on residential buildings, travel agencies opened offices, and the new economy boomed.

3. A Town with a Heart

Overall, Rethymno's so-called "new town" that extends outside of the Venetian walls did not create a violent rupture with the listed settlement inside the walls. Although its appearance is radically different, its scale has remained much the same because of the comparable size of building plots, as well as similar building heights and street width. The bipolarity of this Old and New Town creates strong associations, such as the duel of charming and modern respectively, or of soigné and scruffy. There are, however, other aspects of their coexistence, which will now be looked at.

3.1 A National Matter of Domesticity

In post-war Greece, the state did not provide sufficient support for the strategic growth of the provinces, since it never implemented profound reforms or established a well-founded industry. Nevertheless, Athens went through a long period of economic and construction growth and became the centre of an expanding government. This prosperity partially silenced dissatisfaction with living conditions in urban dwellings. However, the dominance of Athens was not unreservedly welcomed in the smaller towns of Greece. A good example is the case of Rethymno, where, in view of the lack of reforms on their island, Cretans viewed the concentration of authority, capital and growth in Athens as "both political patronage and unemployment relief."[24]

Over the last six decades, the government has been seen by Cretans as merely a distant source of pocket money. In 1960, for example, a Rethemniot newspaper optimistically announced the investment of sig-

---

24 Leland G. Allbaugh, *Crete: a case study of an underdeveloped area* (Princeton, N.J.: University Press 1953), 21.

nificant funds for the construction of public works on the island whereby "the province's isolation and the isolated villages will disappear."[25] The reasons behind Rethymno's particular sense of abandonment also have to do with its antagonistic relationship to the island's major cities, Heraklion and Chania, which continued to attract the labour force that did not migrate to Athens.[26] As a result, until the 1970s, Rethymno was still being depopulated.

Rethymno also faced the drawback of not having a modern, efficient port. Clashes between local interests and opposition to the official plan, disputes over whether the new docks should be located on the eastern or western side of the old port, and the question of sandbars, went on for three decades. Thus, situated between the major commercial centres of Chania and Heraklion, mentioned above, which were already efficiently serving marine and air traffic, Rethymno felt itself to be both overshadowed and overlooked.

Rethymno's sense of abandonment can be further understood by a glimpse into the housing provision initiatives and the Editors' Association Lottery.[27] Apart from monetary prizes, the Lottery often awarded apartments to winners, which, interestingly, were not situated in Rethymno. Instead, they were in Athens, where construction was at its peak, as was the arrival of internal migrants. The message was clear. Winning the lottery meant the chance to get out of the small town and into the capital city. Modern, well-equipped housing was available only five kilometres away from the Acropolis; the provinces had to wait.

3.2 Forgoing modernity

Relatively speaking, Rethymno is not only a small scale city, but its configuration never adapted to the needs of a contemporary municipality and instead retained a 19th century structure. This is in pattern with many towns around the Mediterranean Sea, whose small-scale urban

---

25 "Eparhiaki Ellas" [Provincial Greece], *Kritiki Epitheorisi* (7 February 1960).

26 For example, in 1967, Crete's first cement plant was set up in Heraklion, with the goal of producing 1,500 tons per day. "Ergostasio tsimenton me imerisia paragogi 1,500 tonnon tha idrythi sto Irakleion" [A Cement Plant with a Daily Production of 1,500 Tons Will Be Founded in Heraklion], *Rethemniotika Nea* (4 December 1966).

27 The Lottery operated from the 1930s until 1967. The phenomenon of the lottery and the distribution of apartments as prizes is further addressed in: Yannis Skopeteas – Dimitris Philippidis, *In Exchange for Five Apartments and One Shop!* (Benaki Museum 2005). Also: Ioanna Theocharopoulou, *Urbanization and the Emergence of the Polykatoikìa. Habitat and identity, Athens 1830–1974* (New York: Columbia University 2007).

fabrics were set at the beginning of the 20th century. When entering the modern era, such settlements could continue to function effectively only by preserving this dense, minimal arrangement. At the same time, a large number of such towns did not reach urban maturity, with density being counterbalanced by planning inefficiency, and remained rural until the post-war era.

The peculiar nature of Greek towns arose from an absence of competent planning on the part of the state, as well as from desultory reaction to migratory waves. In the outskirts of Greek cities, settlers occupied state-owned land and built unauthorized homes with no preventive or punitive action taken by the authorities owing to a lack of resources. Unable to offer a formal solution, the government remained silent, as Social Geography Professor Thomas Maloutas suggested, "what happened was a subdivision of large properties that were aimed for usages other than housing, such as horticulture. After this fragmentation, illegal settlements were built, but they were tolerated."[28] This also happened in Rethymno, where municipal planning was in such disorder that it was possible to have individual plots integrated into the city plan despite the fact that they had been built on illegally, as happened in the 1920s. Citizens grew accustomed to ignoring the role of the state, and therefore failed to realize the importance of coherent planning. Instead, they learned to focus on how to speculate on their property, ignoring the lack of infrastructure, roads and transportation this problematic integration would cause.

As a consequence, no zoning was ever realized in Rethymno, whose tissue consists of a haphazard juxtaposition of buildings for housing, commerce, service and tourism purposes, since rational land usage necessarily succumbed to the pressures of urban space restriction. Moreover, the small scale nature of individual enterprises came hand in glove with a lack of sufficient public amenities, such as parks and adequate pavements, and also with problems of hygiene. This has particularly burdened life in the Old Town, where living conditions in the neighbourhoods built in mediaeval times became intolerable. "In a town where house-proud women and fiercely independent men resent the intervention of bureaucratic archaeologists, this devaluation of antiquity symbolically reinforces the general distress that residents express at the physical dirt

---

28 Thomas Maloutas, "Athens before the socio-demographic challenges in the beginning of the 21st century," in *2010 Hamburg, La Fabrique de la Cité (Groupe VINCI)*, Proceedings of the conference The city is alive, Hamburg 2010, 12. Translated from French by the author.

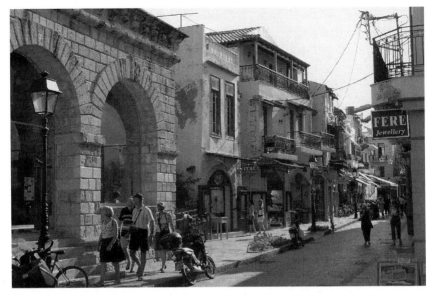

Fig. 3: The now busy streets of Petychaki and Arkadiou are framed by the juxtaposition of Venetian houses. This nobles' meeting point in the 16th century is nowadays known as Loggia (left). Photo: Olga Moatsou, 2016.

which crumbling, damp-ridden walls imposes upon them."[29] Considering the deficient infrastructure and the non-existent separation of levels of nuisance, Rethymno's urban fabric never crossed paths with modernity.

3.3 The Old Town and Musealization

When tourism began growing throughout Greece, the Ministry of Coordination issued a Regional Development Plan for Crete, which urged an examination of the island's perspectives and the undertaking of studies for specific areas. Together with the creation of a Service for the Regional Development of Crete, it clearly promoted thorough planning and an implementation of tourist facilities. This came at a crucial point, since Athens was suffocating and there was widespread concern for its mistakes not to be repeated elsewhere. The completed plans were published in the second issue of the periodical *Architecture in Greece* in 1968, and focused on a more humanistic approach to urban development, on opening and

---

29 Herzfeld, *A Place in History*, 226.

Fig. 4: The mosque and the New Town: Veli Pasha çami. Photo: Olga Moatsou, 2016.

enhancing tourist areas, as well as on a first attempt to introduce sustainability values.

However, in the case of new Rethymno, the programme was implemented with revisions and amendments to the plans, rather than based on their full realization. This has served to emphasize the difference between the two parts of Rethymno, since activities in the Old Town were much better monitored. In contrast to the New Town, where a hands-on management of public space is in practice, in the Old Town it is the municipal authorities, the archaeological service, and the state authorities who supervise changes in building facades, pavements, and facilities. The spatial expansion of the Old Town is also impossible, since its boundaries are clearly defined. Post-war sectors, on the other hand, have sprawled and may well continue to do so, being only partially restricted by the law and by topography.

The small urban scale also proved to be very convenient for the exploitation of tourist resources; the picturesque is profitable. In other words, in the new buildings one could integrate tourist accommodation, without any shift to a larger scale or to creating a significant rupture with the Old Town. In this regard, interestingly, the new town became an uninterrupted extension of the old, touristically profitable one. On the other hand, the new town is not as well-maintained, since it relies on the historical districts to get government attention; indeed, protection of its attractiveness is at the heart of its own economic prosperity and liveliness. However, the Old Town is also a bane, since it is the recipient not only of significant financial support from the European Union, but also of the numerous restrictions that come with this support, such as building preservation and the maintenance of historic features. For this reason, it has caused mixed feelings, as it has become an extended museum for the hordes of tourists, a beautified, prestigious, and noble monument of the past, but one in which strict rules have been laid down.

Another factor that contributes to the disengagement of residents with their town is the constant rotation of population from summer to winter and vice versa. The number of permanent residents is relatively high and stable throughout the year (a trait that does not apply to other Greek tourist towns), but the heavy influx of tourists in the summer is matched by the corresponding arrival of students in the winter. Crete's touristic product is mostly marketed for the summertime, in spite of the great possibilities for recreational activities during the colder months. The departure of holiday-makers in September more or less coincides with the beginning of the academic year and the arrival of students. On the one hand, this maintains the town's vitality, but on the other it intensifies local perceptions of Rethymno as a grand patchwork of temporary accommodation.

3.4 Globalisation and European Identity

The city of Rethymno displays a series of contradictions relative to the rudimentary stage of modernity of the Greek provinces. It is an amalgam of local traditions and European inheritance. The Venetian buildings are properly preserved and promoted as a noble remnant of a glorious past, but contemporary Rethymno presents a conflicting identity. All that is Venetian is praised: "Rethemnos is exemplary of a tendency to conflate all earlier styles as a celebration of European identity through the spread of an increasingly stylized image of European power."[30] However, the religious suppression, heavy taxation and other forms of authoritarian

---

30   Herzfeld, *A Place in History*, 15.

control that accompanied the first years of Venetian rule are ignored. The subsequent Cretan Renaissance overshadows those memories and strengthens the eminence of the Old Town's historical nucleus. Thus, the city acquires a much-desired monumental dimension which emphasizes its relation to European finesse.

With regard to Ottoman times, however, the city's collective perception looks back on this period as an oppressive and, on the whole, negative experience, despite the fact that the daily life of the inhabitants was often quite tolerable. The Ottoman identity of Rethymno was ultimately rejected in the 1920s, with the arrival of the migrants from Turkey. During the waves of population exchange an element of discrepancy was created that went hand-in-hand with a reinvention of national identity. "Like a magnet, the era of the 'yoke of foreign domination' attracts the blame for almost every ill manifested in Greek society. But like all nationalist myths, this one is largely an invented tradition."[31] In line with this trend, Crete had to become entirely Greek and all that was even remotely related to its Ottoman past was discarded.

The attitude towards the city's architectural heritage further underlines Rethymno's preference for its "European" and "Venetian" past. Preservation activities have mainly focused on the Venetian monuments and have often ignored those built in the years of the Ottoman occupation. For instance, the existence of the Muslim cemetery was erased from the city's fabric once the municipal garden was created above it. In addition, one of the city's minarets is at the centre of a long debate concerning its restoration, which was halted five years ago. The fact that Ottoman buildings were often constructed of wood, a less long-lasting material than the stone preferred by the Venetians, has not helped in maintaining or replacing bay windows and shutters.

4. Thoughts on a Small Town

Rethymno does not only identify with its old town. Since the growth and construction boom, however, the new town is commonly belittled by inhabitants. In the 1980s, a journalist in the local press condemned the "inhuman" modern city; "What will our children have to remember?" he wrote. His exclamation ultimately pertains to the appropriation of selective historic layers and to the fact that its international inheritance

---

31 Thomas W. Gallant, *Modern Greece* (London: Arnold 2001), 1.

and monumentality have been necessary to affirm Rethymno's position among larger cities. What is more, this has also had clear effects on the domestic milieu.

On the one hand, with the old town becoming a magnet for tourist development, new neighbourhoods are forced to develop outside its borderline and then sprawl outwards, away from the main economic and administrative centre. On the other, "historic conservation turns the makeshift familiarity of domestic space into something permanent and inelastic."[32] An old town declared to be a historical heritage is automatically transformed into a rigid core that becomes detached from its inhabitants. This occurs through the imposition of laws that restrict construction activities and regulate building morphologies. There is also the high cost and complexity involved in carrying out construction work, since the mere transportation of materials becomes more expensive and machinery has difficulty accessing the narrow, medieval streets. Old buildings are not only difficult and costly to renovate, they are expensive to heat since no central heating can be installed,[33] and they are also affected by the high cost of petroleum.

To sum up, Rethymno turned from an important city of the Venetian state into a small and less significant town of the Modern Greek state. It owes this insignificance to its geographical location on an island and the current dynamics of being overshadowed because of its position between the larger cities of Heraklion and Chania. Looking back on its glory under Venetian rule, contemporary Rethymno draws on its past in order to affirm itself. Nevertheless, its relationship with the bygone era is also passive-aggressive, alternating between pride and admiration at one point to scorn at another. Rethemniots appreciate the benefits of a restored and well-maintained old town, but they also feel a certain degree of asphyxiation because of the rigidity that the rules of preservation impose. In order to address this vicious circle of emotions and identity confusion, a further investigation of Rethymno's historic development and the reasons for the emotional rollercoaster it has engendered are necessary. At least, however, small towns are now closer to the foreground of theoretical debate.

---

32 Herzfeld, *A Place in History*, 58.
33 Rethemniotis (pen-name), "Rethemniotikes kouventes," [Rethemniot Conversations] *Kritiki Epitheorisi* (25 January 1969).

Miraculous Equilibrium. Keys for a Sustainable Network of Small South Iberian Cities
Blanca Del Espino Hidalgo

1. Introduction

This research aims to make a wide, transversal analysis of a territorial and urban phenomenon that has for centuries shaped a set of small cities that currently comprise sixty percent of the land structure in the southern part of the Iberian Peninsula, and which are still growing in terms of urban land and population.

It focuses on two main topics. On the one hand, it is a study of a dense collection of human settlements and their evolution from the 19th century to the present as they changed from huge agricultural centres of production to new industrial, tourist and services' poles, including an analysis of the creative/destructive variations in urban, architectonic, agricultural, industrial and ethnological heritage indices. On the other, urban, economic and demographic growth variables, in terms of both the cities themselves and their reciprocal influence on the small rural settlements in their environs, are examined.

This comparative study of two urban networks, in close proximity geographically but functionally very distant, which for spatial reasons will be typified by a small city from each, demonstrates the deep influence of land-planning and urban-management strategies on the fate of small cities in general. It also shows the power of heritage and historical bonds to generate long-lasting territorial equilibrium and sees in these cities the key to successful development in the southern part of the Iberian Peninsula.

2. Conceptual Framework

At the outset, the strong links between the concepts of "heritage" and "sustainability" should be considered. The term "heritage" occurred for the first time in the law of the Roman Republic and referred to the property of patricians that was inherited from generation to generation within a family.[1] Later, the use of the word became widespread, keeping its original sense but adding a very common second one: the set of cultural goods that a culture owns. Thus, our understanding of the word today combines both features: on the one hand, an appreciation of the assets received and, on the other, an image of what we, in turn, will pass on to our descendants. The expression "sustainable development" – nowadays obsolete and replaced by "sustainability" – was originally coined for the report entitled: "Our common future", as "development that meets the needs of the present without compromising the ability of future generations to meet their own needs."[2]

In terms of meaning, therefore, both concepts refer to something we receive, take care of and, in due course, pass on. In this respect, a sense of legacy and continuity is conveyed, together with that of guardianship, responsibility, and conscience. This leads to the idea that, practically speaking, heritage embodies the roots of sustainability or, in other words, that heritage itself is sustainable.

3. Small Cities as a Case Study

Studies of small cities have not been the subject of research in a European context for some time. In the southern part of the Iberian Peninsula, however, treatment of the topic has been seen as a means of understanding territorial and urban structures. In recent decades, these city networks have acquired an increasing role in academic discourse, owing both to interest in their place within the urban category, and to the role they play in the territories of Andalusia and Alentejo.

1 Friedrich Engels, *La gens y el estado en Roma. El origen de la familia, la propiedad privada y el estado VI* (Madrid: Alianza Editorial 2008).
2 Gro Harlem Brundtland et alii, *Brutndtland Report. Our common future* (Oxford: Oxford University Press 1987).

3.1 Definition and Relevance of Small Cities in Research

A terminological discussion, initiated as early as 1984, is still current. In a study of twenty-nine Latin American scientific journals published from 1972 to 1984, the need for a deeper study of small cities, a theme which was virtually absent from the academic world, was found to have been voiced.[3] During the last thirty years, work on the problematic nature of this category of urban settlements has proliferated, mainly in Latin America and Europe. Present in all of these has been the question of small and medium-size cities, which have been compared and contrasted on a worldwide scale. Indeed, ironically, they have even been defined as unidentified geographic objects (UGOs).[4]

Most commentators agree in defining the small cities in the southern part of the Iberian Peninsula as medium-sized. The criteria are twofold: on the one hand, scale – absolute and relative with regard to territorial context – and, on the other, their functional role within the territory. In terms of quantitative standards, the categorizing of small and intermediate cities has been diverse, depending not just on particular urban traditions but also on significant differences among authors studying cities even within the same country or region. For Europe, the range has been established as, between 20,000 and 50,000 inhabitants, approximately.[5]

In this sense, the setting of numeric limits would correspond not to the geographic location, nor to the local population relative to the national one, but to much more varied rationalisation – so much so that the majority of the characteristics according to which small or intermediate cities are defined today emerge from eliminating and discarding other options in comparison with the bigger urban settlements. These features are generally positive: urban systems are more balanced and sustainable; their relationship to the territory is more harmonious; urban

---

3   Carmen Bellet and Josep Maria Llop, "Miradas a otros espacios urbanos: las ciudades intermedias," *Scripta Nova Geo Crítica, revista electrónica de geografía y ciencias sociales* 8, no. 165 (2004); Carrión Mena, Fernando, "Poder local y ciudades intermedias," *IV Congreso Nacional de Sociología,* Quito (Ecuador: Puce 1986), as cited in José Castillo Palma and Elisa Patiño Tovar, "Ciudades medias," *Elementos, Ciencia y Cultura* 6, no. 34, (1999), 29–33, Puebla: Universidad Autónoma de Puebla.

4   Carmen Bellet and Josep Maria Llop, *Ciudades intermedias y urbanización mundial* (Lleida: UNESCO, Ayuntament de Lleida, UIA, Ministerio de Asuntos Exteriores 1999).

5   Andrés Rojas, "Las ciudades medias y la expansión territorial," *La Ciudad Viva.* [Online]. Friday, 23rd October 2009. http://www.laciudadviva.org/blogs/?p=2895 (accessed 1. 7. 2014).

centres are easier to manage and govern; the scale of the settlements stimulates strong feelings of identity; and they lead to fewer environmental problems and social conflict. On the other hand, there are also some disadvantages such as less sociocultural diversity, a certain amount of social endogamy, little economic competition and more difficult access to information and capital.[6]

In sum, with regard to their consideration in this present work, the definition of small cities in the southern part of the Iberian Peninsula is based on the identification of an urban entity which, midway between big cities and rural regions, constitutes a secondary centre whose role is to serve a variety of minor or similar settlements, and which lacks the typical infrastructure of a metropolitan or central urban area.

3.2 Networks of Small Cities in the Southern Part of the Iberian Peninsula

As already mentioned, small cities are commonly defended as more sustainable human settlements in economic, environmental and, particularly, social terms. Indeed, European guidelines expressly recommend the encouragement of intermediate centres as a model for the future development of the urban world.[7] In that sense, the sustainability of these cities depends, on the one hand, on a matter of scale – they must be large enough to contain the means for satisfaction of most urban activities without a need to move to major urban areas or capitals – and, on the other, on their location within the territory in comparison with other centres, since they usually provide basic services for the inhabitants of smaller towns and villages around them. In other words, through their networking, infrastructure and tertiary sector elements, they can fulfil the majority of the functions of urban facilities, within a relatively minor commuting distance; and, furthermore, in their more basic functions, they play a centralising role for a good number of smaller settlements.[8]

Henceforth, when considering these cities as a matter or source of sustainability, it will be necessary to address them not as isolated urban elements but rather as parts of a net which, established throughout the territory, have the ability to modify and also be modified by their

---

6   See Carmen. Bellet – Josep Maria Llop, *Ciudades intermedias y urbanización mundial*.

7   European Commission, *Cities for Tomorrow* (Brussels: Council of Europe 2011).

8   José María Feria Toribio et alii, *El sistema urbano andaluz. Aglomeraciones urbanas, áreas de centralidad y ámbitos desarticulados* (Sevilla: Instituto de Desarrollo Regional, Consejería de Obras Públicas y Transportes 1992).

constraints, and inside which they interact with one another and find a position of equilibrium that justifies their role as secondary centres in the system as a whole. For this reason, before proceeding to a more detailed approach to the selected small cities as case studies, which will lead to reflections on their sustainability, it is useful to bear in mind some key considerations regarding their territorial determination, taking into account the fact that their own definition as a set, as well as the defence of the sustainability of their urban scale, comes from a particular position inside a territorial hierarchy and their fixed role with regard to other settlements with major or minor relevance to their context.[9]

To analyse the urban, territorial and landscaping sustainability of small cities in the southern part of the Iberian Peninsula, we have chosen two subject areas with sizes of about 30,000 square kilometres each (approximately the size of Belgium) in two regions which, due to their particularities, correspond in an exemplary way to the conditions given in the definition of this urban category, and which possess a valuable historical legacy, inherited from their position as secondary centres over many centuries.

In addition, the networks of both the small cities, POTA in Andalusia, Spain, and PROT Alentejo in Portugal, have been recognised by the official land planning agencies in both regions and earmarked as key sets in terms of urban balance achievement and rural development opportunities. Furthermore, different but comparable interlinking and heritage-based initiatives to promote regional growth have arisen in the two, primarily with respect to tourism, which reveal the potential of history to strengthen the bonds between urban settlements and to generate development within traditionally poor areas.

Their characterization as networks must be understood, however, not just as a result of official acknowledgement and encouragement in order to attract economic prosperity but, more fundamentally, with regard to their functioning in relation to one another and also to the rural areas around them. In this sense, their role as intermediate centres for relatively extensive areas has been reinforced by official policies in implementing essential public services, on the basis of complementarity and interdependency. This can easily be checked by consulting the requisite land planning documents. Thus, public facilities such as hospitals, judicial districts, railway junctions and highway connections are distributed among the urban cores in such a way that every citizen in the region can

---

9   *Plan de Ordenación Territorial de Andalucía (POTA)*, Title II, Section 2, 2006.

have easy access to all within a short time.[10] This fact can be explained not just from the perspective of territorial policy, but also from an understanding of the competitive nature of the inhabitants of the cities in question, who have repeatedly stressed their demands, and even resorted to demonstrations, when the allocation of a new service was at stake. This statement can be extended to include the decision-making processes in the location of private services, namely large commercial and logistics centres, as well as to areas with a particularly high concentration of specialized professional services.

Regarding landscape – understood not just as a pictorial or visual entity but rather as the summa of natural and human actions throughout the territory[11] – the networking functioning of both sets of small cities has been historically reinforced by shared identities: firstly, their traditional connection with the rural and agricultural worlds grouped them in large landscape units and made them adapt not just to the topographic and natural conditions but also to the Mediterranean trilogy crop system of wheat, wines, and olives; secondly, as a result of parallel historical legacies such as defensive structures, similar archaeological sites and clusters of religious buildings were originally owned by the same monastic or mendicant orders. All this has contributed to the birth of networking initiatives, which keep heritage and landscape as their main driving force, and to the resources in both regions, which in addition to cultural tourism also focus on social and cultural development.

Thus, we have drawn attention to two aspects of the reality of two different territorial enclaves that nevertheless share the common presence of a strong network of small cities. Following the principles enumerated at the beginning of this chapter, these facilitate a process of sustainability and equilibrium in the structure of the urban population in each. In addition, contrasts are evident when one compares their spatial shape and configuration as well as their relationship with other smaller or bigger settlements. With such common aspects noted, we can move on to study the more significant characteristics of their territoriality and evolution over recent decades.

---

10   Feria Toribio et alii, *El sistema urbano andaluz.*
11   *European Landscape Convention*, Florence: Council of Europe 2010, available at http://www. coe.int/es/web/landscape (accessed 20. 10. 2015).

4. An Approach to the Territoriality and Evolution of Small Cities in Andalusia and Alentejo

If the urban disposition and hierarchy of the two regions being examined are professedly different, so, too, must be the consideration given to the evolution and the current state of sustainability in their territories. In our study, the two sets will be analysed separately, with the understanding that the political, social, territorial and historical contexts have the ability to predetermine the urban dynamics in such a way as to ensure that they cannot be treated as one and the same case but rather as two complementary and comparable ones.

4.1 Small Cities in the Centre of Andalusia

With respect to the Andalusian set we can affirm that, with diverse origins which stretch from prehistory in some cases, and from the Middle Ages in others (Atlas, 2009), their strategic positioning in the central area of Andalusia is generally associated with the previous existence of historic roads that followed the natural paths between the main urban cores provided by the complex topography of the region. Moreover, the cities included in the study have always been linked to their frontier status, either because they were settled between different units of landscape – the Baetic mountain range, the meadows of Northern Malaga, the countryside of Cordoba and Seville and the inner valley of the Guadalquivir River – or, particularly in the eastern region, due to their historic position between the Christian and Arab kingdoms from the 12th to the 15th centuries, with most being key defensive points and strongholds that repeatedly changed from one side to the other.[12]

This has permitted, over the centuries, the conformation of a network which, in its general outlines, preserves a mostly homogeneous structure in terms of the distance between its main urban cores [see Picture 1] that has benefited its centralising or intermediary function. Such a situation, however, did not proceed from a planned territorial strategy focussed on equidistance but rather from the stepwise emergence of human settlements – which may or may not still remain today – that, currently, configure an apparently balanced network.

---

12 José Díaz Quidiello et alii, *Atlas de la historia del territorio de Andalucía* (Sevilla: Instituto de Cartografía de Andalucía e Instituto Andaluz del Patrimonio Histórico 2009).

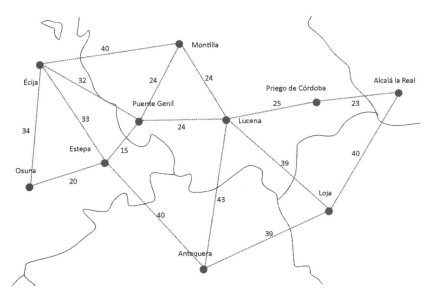

Fig. 1: Network of small cities in Andalusia (author's selection). Distances in kilometres. Source: Prepared by the author on the basis of "Infraestructura de Datos Espaciales de Andalucía (IDEAndalucía)" [Online], 2015. http://www.ideandalucia.es/portal/web/ideandalucia/datos-y-servicios/ideavisor# IDEAvisor/ (accessed 12. 7. 2015).

With regard to land use, Andalusian small cities are characterised by large municipal areas and dense urban cores (average population densities vary from 40 to 100 inhabitants per square kilometre, with about 90% of the population generally living in the main city of the municipality, in densities of from 50 to 80 dwellings per hectare).

Nowadays, such small cities constitute a network that configures most of the regional territory. Nonetheless, publications on the sustainable urban heritage in Andalusia generally refer only to the major cities, and include an area declared as a World Heritage Site by UNESCO, or to rural areas comprising little towns, villages and scattered settlements. However, these small cities possess a special value due to their strategic position around a territorial communications node. Since over the centuries they were rich enclaves of the inner Andalusian lands, they were commonly named "agro-cities," although often in a derogatory sense.[13] In addition, they formed a unique urban phenomenon: settlements with the

---

13   José Luis Díaz Quidiello, "Las ciudades medias interiores en el Plan de Ordenación del Territorio de Andalucía." *Boletín PH* 47 (2007), 44–53.

dimensions of cities but which kept the typical structure of the agricultural world. They were generally linked to a rural system of exploitation based on large land estates, with a clearly segregated social hierarchy and lack of provisional services or facilities proportional to their population. With the passage of time, they have experienced a territorial, urban and even economic valorisation process, which has meant a diversification of the productive sectors and, in some cases, has led to very active emerging industries. In this manner, they have clearly acquired the proper functions of cities and been turned into new opportunity areas for the articulation of the region.[14] This has provided them with a new social and economic dynamism. Since the demographic and productive crisis suffered during the fifties, which was provoked by the depletion of the agricultural system, there has been, instead of agrarian reform, an increase in the variety of niche markets. In addition, due probably to the strategic position of the area regarding opportunities for providing road connections, small and large-size industries have been created without a clear connection to previous traditional activities. In the eighties, this trend became stronger and partially superseded the agricultural sector as the socioeconomic base, making use of the term "agro-city," although outdated as a definition for this urban phenomenon.[15] Moreover, the new urban functions required and were reinforced by a noticeable increase in the services sector, which today accounts for at least 50% of the jobs in each of the cities studied and, in some, up to 70%.[16]

It is not possible, however, to understand this change without considering the territorial transformation that took place simultaneously with it. In this regard, we can identify two temporal milestones. The first is the decommissioning of a great part of the medium-distance railway network, which was particularly dense in the case of Andalusia,[17] due to a critical situation in the National Network of Spanish Railways (Red Nacional de Ferrocarriles Españoles, RENFE) in 1984. The second milestone coincided chronologically with the first one. In 1985, the new

14 *Plan de Ordenación Territorial de Andalucía (POTA)*, 2006.

15 Inmaculada Caravaca, et al., *Innovación y Territorio. Análisis comparado de Sistemas Productivos Locales en Andalucía* (Sevilla: Consejería de Economía y Hacienda, Colección Pablo de Olavide, Junta de Andalucía 2002).

16 Instituto De Estadística De Andalucía, *Atlas estadístico de Andalucía* (Sevilla: Junta de Andalucía, 2010) http://www.juntadeandalucia.es/institutodeestadisticaycartografia./atlas/publicacion /index.html (accessed 26. 10. 2015).

17 See David Lentisco, *Cuando el hierro se hace camino, historia del ferrocarril en España* (Madrid: Alianza Editorial 2005), and Horacio Capel, "Ferrocarril, territorio y ciudades," *Revista Bibliográfica de Geografía y Ciencias Sociales* 12, no. 717 (2007).

national roads plan was approved, with the inclusion of motorways (high-speed roads without the need to pay a toll, as had normally occurred) as the principal focus.[18] The urban reaction to the new backbone axes was immediate. Those historically stable cores, in terms of their dimensions, linked to the small agrarian estates around them in a basic system of primary provisioning, started to increase in area in a significant, nonconcentric way, and sought connectivity with the main forms of transport in order to promote economic development. It is thus our understanding that the process by which agro-cities were converted into small industrial and service sector cities followed, to a large extent, from the development of the infrastructure.

This has undoubtedly brought great advantages in terms of social sustainability, among which we can identify a generally positive demographic evolution, with some minor exceptions, that confirms the existence of a population permanently linked to the small cities [Table 1] despite the decline of the Andalusian agrarian model.

As a result, their agricultural identity has had a powerful impact on the rural landscape, which is divided into several landscape units that correspond to the official administrative districts: Sevilla Countryside, Cordoba Countryside, Subbetic and Jaen Mountains, and Antequera and Archidona Meadows.[19] Although geographical features between units are different, all share some landscape similarities, particularly those related to the predominant crops, which are usually olive trees, frequently cereals and, more rarely, vineyards or vegetable gardens.

Regarding urban heritage, they share some common elements inherited from their historic genesis. Significant archaeological sites exist, since most were secondary urban centres during the Roman Empire or even in Proto-History. There are castles and large fortifications which for more than two centuries marked the frontier between the Muslim and Christian territories in the Middle Ages, also craft industries (e.g. ceramics) that vary from city to city in terms of materials and decoration but share the same shapes and domestic functions.

However, both the social structure and the urban landscape have suffered, together with the evolution of the economic system, from an erosion of their main values, which has seriously affected the sustain-

---

18   Justo Borrajo Sebastián, *La Ley de Carreteras y su reglamento* (Madrid: Dirección General de Carreteras, Ministerio de Fomento 2006).

19   Instituto Andaluz del Patrimonio Histórico, *Paisajes y patrimonio cultural en Andalucía. Tiempo, usos e imágenes* (2 Vol.), PH cuadernos, no. 27 (Sevilla: Junta de Andalucía 2010).

Table 1: Demographic evolution of small cities in inner Andalusia. Source: prepared by the author on the basis of databases from the 1857 Spanish census – "Censo de la Población de España"; 1970 Spanish census – "Censo de la Población de España – Tomo II –Volúmenes Provinciales"; and the 2011 Spanish census – "Censo de Población y Viviendas 2011."

Province	District	City	Population		
			1857	1970	2011
Sevilla	Campiña de Carmona	Carmona	18 799	24 599	28 679
	Campiña de Morón y Marchena	El Viso del Alcor	5 325	11 293	18 828
		Mairena del Alcor	4 493	10 444	21 560
		Arahal	9 911	16 103	19 382
		Morón de la Frontera	15 806	30 029	28 489
		Marchena	13 005	21 180	19 891
	Comarca de Écija	Écija	28 759	36 106	40 718
	Sierra sur de Sevilla	Osuna	17 480	21 466	17 973
		Estepa	9 089	9 803	12 637
Córdoba	Campiña sur de Córdoba	Puente Genil	9 764	26 701	30 424
	Campiña de Montilla	Montilla	14 654	22 469	23 870
	Campiña de Baena	Baena	13 291	20 073	21 028
	Subbética	Cabra	12 891	20 722	21 188
		Lucena	17 057	27 978	42 560
		Priego de Córdoba	14 162	21 541	23 528
Jaén	Sierra sur de Jaén	Alcalá la Real	14 207	22 024	22 758
Málaga	Comarca de Antequera	Antequera	27 340	41 276	41 854
Granada	Comarca de Loja	Loja	17 128	21 865	21 618

Instituto Nacional de Estadística de España [Online] www.ine.es (accessed 12. 7. 2015).

ability of their cultural heritage and identity. Vernacular features have been replaced by Neo-Baroque decoration, simplicity by ostentation,[20] while a large number of small heritage elements that conformed dense

20   Víctor Fernández Salinas, "Paisaje urbano en las ciudades medias," *Boletín PH* 63 (2007), 54–61.

and uniform historic centres into a sort of collective intelligence have been supplanted by new buildings, which have the clear aim of creating an image of economic progress, but often fail when it comes to valuing and making known monuments or immaterial signifiers of heritage.[21] Thus, a social, economic and demographic evolution – although it has had a positive influence on some aspects of the equilibrium of the small Andalusian cities – has adversely affected others, especially in the fields of heritage and culture.

On the other hand, official discourse in recent years has been concerned with defending the common heritage as a resource for territorial and urban development, as well as with the shared aim of building a network of small Andalusian cities. Especially noteworthy are the initiatives in respect of the cultural routes between settlements that have a particular relevance to a historic period or, more successfully, the network known as *Ciudades Medias del Centro de Andalucía*, a mainly private foundation in which seven local governments are working together to enhance cultural tourism in the area. Other public policies have been initiated to support agro-industries and gastronomic tourism, with strong territorial and networking components.

Let us now consider what has occurred with their Portuguese counterparts.

4.2 Small Cities in Alentejo

The agglomeration of small cities in the region of Alentejo forms an urban and territorial reality complementary to that in the centre of Andalusia with regard to diverse factors such as the size of the municipalities, in terms of both population and surface area. The Alentejo towns are similar to or slightly smaller than their Andalusian counterparts, with comparable densities inside the urban cores, although considerably higher in their rural environs. Furthermore, the distances between the different nodes of the network appear appreciably larger than those in Andalusia. With respect to urban morphology and the relationship between the main core and the rest of the city, their historic centres are relatively big, with some urban expansion for residential, industrial and tertiary sector areas. They are generally linked to the main infrastructural systems – whose stronger lineal elements support the presence of the cities with a greater weight

---

21 Antonio Muñoz Martínez, "El Plan Turístico de Ciudades Medias: el interior avanza," *Boletín PH* 63 (2007), 70–74.

within the network – and include diverse landscape units in a relatively small territorial demarcation.[22]

Moreover, in a country whose urban reality is largely polarised,[23] with more than half of the national population settled in the metropolitan areas of Lisbon or Porto, the forty small cities – as counted by the official documents[24] – are seen, both in the academic sphere and by administrative documents pertaining to land planning, as attractive spaces full of opportunities for the future demographic readjustment of Portuguese territory.[25] As a result, a sizeable number of redevelopment, development and investment programmes have been and are being applied. The goal of these programmes has been to bring inhabitants from heavily populated and rural areas closer to the small cities, whose scattering makes sustainable management and growth difficult.[26]

Peripheral conditions in the country – not only regarding physical but also particularly social and economic distance – have, on the other hand, encouraged a sense of urban and territorial identity that is reinforced by the size of the urban communities. Furthermore, we have to consider the idiosyncrasies of the Portuguese territorial administration, which turns every urban settlement of a certain size in relation to its surroundings into a small capital city with respect to a portion of territory that is called a *concelho* (council). For this reason, in addition to the natural evolution provided by demographic growth, each of the small cities studied in the Alentejo also acts as a small services centre.

Nevertheless, when first addressing the territorial approach to the networks of small cities in Alentejo [Fig. 2], one notices that their own spatial configuration has been established in a very different way from their Andalusian homologues, particularly regarding matters of homogeneity and isotropy. The strong presence of the Elvas-Vendas Novas axis, corresponding both physically and functionally with the Lisbon-Madrid axis, marks a predominantly linear structure with transversal lines that go in opposite directions – Sines and Beja to the south and Portalegre to the north.

---

22 *Plan Regional de Ordenación del Territorio del Alentejo* (PROT Alentejo 2010).

23 Teresa Sá Marques et al., *Sistema Urbano Nacional. Cidades médias e dinâmicas territoriais*. 2 vol. (Lisboa: Direcção-Geral do Ordenamento do Território e Desenvolvimento Urbano 1997).

24 *Despachos* of the MPAT 6/7 (PROSIURB 1994).

25 Ana Mafalda Rodrigues, *Regulação urbanística e forma da nova expansão urbana: o caso de Évora*. [Online] (Coimbra: Universidade de Coimbra 2006). http://hdl.handle.net/10316/6003 (accessed 24. 9. 2014).

26 Ricardo Manuel do Carmo, "Cidades médias. Do crescimento demográfico à consolidação territorial," *Cidades – Comunidades e Territórios* 12/13 (2006), 69–82.

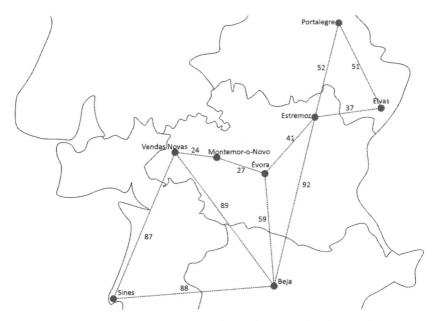

Fig. 2: Network of small cities in Alentejo (author's selection). Distances in kilometres. Source: Prepared by the author on the basis of "Carta Administrativa Oficial de Portugal-CAOP2014" [Online], 2015. http://mapas.dgterritorio.pt /viewer/index.html (accessed 12. 7. 2015).

Municipal areas in Alentejo are generally large (average population densities vary from 30 to 80 inhabitants per square kilometre), although the percentage of inhabitants living in the main urban core is considerably lower than in Andalusia (about 60%). Urban densities, on the other hand, are slightly larger in Andalusia than in the inner settlements of Alentejo (with in general urban densities of 40 to 70 dwellings per hectare).

Although it has been traditionally known as the poorest region in Portugal, Alentejo has a solid urban and territorial heritage in the network of small cities described, sharing this feature with the small cities in inner Andalusia. Furthermore, this characteristic suggests a certain unity between the two regions which, from a geographical point of view, possess a clear distinctiveness based, as previously seen, not just on their physical characteristics but also on their historic identity.

In terms of demography and land planning, as noted earlier, these settlements have been identified over decades as providing great op-

Table 2: Demographic evolution of small cities in the south of Portugal (regions of Alentejo and Algarve). Source: prepared by the author on the basis of databases from the 1864 Portuguese census – "I Recenseamento Geral da População"; 1970 Portuguese census – "XI Recenseamento Geral da População"; and 2011 Portuguese census – "XV Recenseamento Geral da População."

Region	Province	City	Population		
			1864	1970	2011
Alentejo	Bajo Alentejo	Beja	6 874	24 180	30 470
	Alto Alentejo	Elvas	10 271	22 230	23 078
		Portalegre	6 433	25 800	24 930
	Alentejo Central	Évora	11 518	27 935	30 470
	Alentejo Litoral	Sines	*	7 550	13 200
Algarve	Barlovento	Lagos	7 744	16 550	22 095
		Portimão	*	25 585	45 431
	Sotavento	Faro	8 014	30 535	44 119
		Olhão	*	9 850	14 914

Instituto Nacional de Estadística de Portugal [Online] https://www.ine.pt/ (accessed 12. 7. 2015).
* Note: the 1864 Census just included the populations of the cities that were considered, at that moment, to be urban settlements. The remainder are supposed to be included in the corresponding districts.

portunities to re-balance a population system that has gradually tended to be polarising between rural areas and big cities.[27] This process has been particularly dramatic in the southern part of the country,[28] due to the fact that it has repeatedly been the subject of urban regeneration initiatives.[29]

At this point, we can highlight the PROSIURB Programme for the Consolidation of the Urban System and Support for the Implementation of Local Masterplans (*Programa de Consolidação do Sistema Urbano Nacional e Apoio* à *Execução dos Planos Diretores Municipais*), developed between 1994 and 1997, which, in addition to the investment of material and human resources in the urban consolidation of these municipalities, defined the concept and relevance of Portuguese small cities as interme-

---

27 João Ferrao, "Rede urbana portuguesa: uma visão internacional," *Janus* (2001), 52–57.
28 See Sá Marques et alii, *Sistema Urbano Nacional* (1997).
29 See Eduarda Marques da Costa, "Uma nota sobre as políticas das cidades em Portugal nos anos noventa," *Inforgeo* 14 (Lisboa: Edições Colibri 1999), 131–137.

diate centres for the first time.[30] This programme was followed by the POLIS Programme for the Urban Requalification and Environmental Valorisation of Cities (Programa de Requalificação Urbana e Valorização Ambiental de Cidades), launched in 1999 and more focussed on urban and environmental interventions than on planning or conservation policies.[31]

In any event, the main result of these great programmes at the national level, as with those in the inner lands of Andalusia, was the encouragement of stabilisation. Indeed, it even led to a slight increase in population around the intermediate centres in this region located in the south of Portugal. The effect was more noticeable in the bigger towns, while in the smaller ones the population rise was more subtle or even decreased slightly, as can be observed in the case of Portalegre [Table 2].

In a like manner, the development of the urban settlements generally involved the reformulation of the national transportation and communication structures. Thus, the disarticulation of the road system and the obsolescence of the railway system[32] during the nineties drove their reformulation and activated the layout of new ways that were generally overlaid on the original ones. These attempts to reinforce the system have since been unified thanks to the national road plan in 2000 and, more recently, the strategic blueprint for transport and infrastructure in 2014. These initiatives, in turn, have been closely linked, in the southern area, with the promotion and development of cultural tourism in the case of Alentejo.[33] In this context, the construction of the Beja airport and the highway connected to it stand out, although both projects are currently stalled, as are the alternatives to beach tourism in the case of the nearby region of the Algarve.[34] The overlap of the EN-125 national road with the A22 highway, and its further conversion into a tolled roadway should also be mentioned.

These great infrastructural investments have seriously affected, in many ways, the sustainability of the rural landscape, which originally was much more diverse, in terms of the number of units, than its Andalusian counterpart: the small cities studied are settled between eight different landscape units, namely: Tejo and Sado Moorlands, the Lowlands of the

---

30 *Despachos* of the MPAT 6/94 and 7/94 (PROSIURB) (1994).

31 *Despacho* of the MAOT 47/A/99 (POLIS) (1999).

32 Jorge Almeida Santos, "Problemas fundamentais do tráfego e dos transportes em Portugal. Questões estratégicas," *Análise Psicológica* 3, no. 13 (1995), 249–252.

33 *Plan Regional de Ordenación del Territorio del Alentejo (PROTAlentejo)* (2010).

34 *Plan Regional de Ordenación del Territorio del Algarve (PROTAlgarve)* (2007).

High Alentejo, the Marble Area, Pastures, the Surroundings of Évora, the Agricultural Lands of Alqueva, the Littoral-Inner Transition Area, and the Littoral Sandy Lowland.[35]

Apart from those cultural identity features directly linked with rural landscape – oenology and the ethnologic heritage related to agriculture are particularly characteristic of the region – the main common historic elements are strongly connected with those in Andalusia: archaeology – especially significant are the sites that proceed from the Roman Era – and defensive structures – it has to be borne in mind that the Spanish-Portuguese frontiers have changed between the 12th to the 20th centuries.

On both the heritage and landscape fronts, however, action has been less effective and further delayed. In addition to the effects of the PROSI-URB and POLIS programmes regarding the historic fabric of the small cities,[36] the refurbishment of identity, the valorisation and diffusion of labour in the case of the two small cities included in the World Heritage List – Evora in 1985, and Elvas in 2012 – deserve notice. So, too, does the more recent development of catalogues and itineraries by the General Heritage Authority of Portugal. These include some matters concerning the cultural aspects of the landscape units in the land-planning for the Region of Alentejo.

Apart from this, the national cultural administration (IGESPAR) has been developing territorial initiatives, mainly through the implementation of heritage routes with a common historic and typological theme, such as Roman bridges and winery cellars. Their shared efforts to improve the productiveness of cultural tourism in the region should enhance network functioning regarding heritage.

5. Case Studies for an Evaluation of the Heritage and Landscape Equilibrium in the Southern Part of the Iberian Peninsula

As mentioned earlier, in order to study the relationship between heritage and sustainability in terms of the networks of small cities from a territorial-scaled perspective, two sets in two regions of the southern part of the Iberian Peninsula were selected: those in the centre of Andalusia, Spain, and those in Alentejo, Portugal. In line with this arrangement,

---

35 *Plan Regional de Ordenación del Territorio del Alentejo (PROTAlentejo)* (2010).

36 José Aguiar, Antonio Reis Cabrita and João Appleton, *Guião de apoio à reabilitação de edifícios habitacionais* (Lisboa: LNEC 1998).

two cities will be examined in greater detail, Lucena in Andalusia and Beja in Alentejo, as paradigms of the contradictions between economic and urban evolution over the past decades and their social, cultural and environmental equilibrium.

5.1 Lucena

In a way that is analogous to other small cities in the same area, Lucena is located at a historic crossing, an enclave between the north and the south, and the east and the west of Andalusia. It constitutes a unique case in terms of the surrounding socioeconomic environment, which undoubtedly has had major repercussions on its landscape, as it has played the role of an inflection point between two landscape demarcations. In addition, it has, historically, constituted a territorial centre for cultures that were generally scarcely relevant in other Andalusian locations. Moreover, it is currently the most populated of all the small cities in the inner area of Andalusia [Table 1].

This fact stands in marked contrast with the scant protection afforded to the preservation of its heritage, which still contains some very significant components even though the great economic growth experienced during recent decades has led to large-scale destruction of the vernacular architecture [Picture 3]. The majority of these elements come from the legacy of the periods that were particularly relevant to the territory, in particular the Middle Ages and, more specifically, the period when, under the aegis of the Muslim banner, a very large Jewish community constituted the main population in Lucena[37]. This situation continued until the capture in 1483 of King Boabdil – the last Muslim sovereign of the Peninsula – at the hands of the Count of Cabra, Diego III Fernández de Córdoba in the Battle of Martín González, and which led to the expulsion of Muslims and Sephardim from the city. For this reason, it has sparked, in the current century, a re-assessment of this historic period[38], and been responsible for one of the more representative heritage resources at both the level of local identity and in the panorama of tourist revitalisation programmes.[39]

---

37 Joaquín Pérez Azaustre, *Lucena sefardita: la ciudad de los poetas* (Barcelona: Andalucía Abierta 2005).

38 Joan Viciano et al., "A probable case of gigantism/acromegaly in skeletal remains from the Jewish necrópolis of 'Ronda Sur'" (Lucena, Córdoba, Spain; VIII–XII centuries CE)," *Antropologischer Anzeiger* 71, no. 1, (2015), 67–87.

39 Blanca Del Espino et al., "Patrimonio, turismo e identidad en las ciudades medias del centro

Fig. 3: St. Mateo Parish Church in Plaza Nueva, Lucena, as isolated Heritage background of the residential buildings replaced during the 20th Century. Photo: Blanca Del Espino Hidalgo, 2012.

Between the 16th and 18th centuries, Lucena remained a settlement strongly linked to the agrarian world, particularly to olive tree orchards and vineyards and the production of olive oil and wine. In addition, there were strong religious associations which made it the artistic core of the Late Baroque style in Cordoba.[40] From the 19th century, the city gradually acquired its present shape and consolidated itself as a commercial centre thanks to the vigour of two alimentary industries: oil and winegrowing. In the first case, the establishment of a railway network was of fundamental importance for the Subbética region, commonly known as the "Oil Train." It connected the olive production centres in the province of Jaen – with a stop at the city of Martos – with the main modes of transport to the south-western area of Andalusia – Malaga and Seville essentially – and passed through the majority of the municipalities of the Subbética, including Lucena. This industrialisation increased during the 20th century, by the end of which the city had been turned into the second national production centre of wood furniture and the

de Andalucía," in *Turismo en Andalucía y el norte de Marruecos: nuevos retos, nuevas propuestas*, (Málaga: ConecturMED, 2014).

40   Jesús Rivas Carmona, *Arquitectura barroca cordobesa* (Córdoba: Monte de Piedad y Caja de Ahorros de Córdoba 1982).

first for industrial cooling.[41] During this period, the service sector also developed, and up to the present has coexisted with the industrial and agrarian sectors as the main source of employment. Both the oil and wine industries provide numerous examples of agrarian architecture as a territorial legacy – e.g., farmhouses dispersed along the olive lands and several urban and peri-urban wine cellars – which today remain in varying conditions of use and conservation.

Despite the fact that its historic centre is one of the largest within the panorama of the small Andalusian cities, it has only seven historic buildings protected at the highest level in the official heritage catalogue (Bien de Interés Cultural), six of which are inside the historic core (including the Historic Area itself, whose file was initiated in 1972 and has never been completed). The remainder include a castle, a palace, two churches and an old convent-hospital. The only listed building located outside the urban fabric is an archaeological site that includes proto-historic to medieval strata and is currently abandoned, lacking both a basic enclosure and protective maintenance. The more mundane heritage is composed mostly of traditional dwellings and some examples of religious and aristocratic architecture, with a total number of 195 buildings protected within the remit of the local urban planning authority.

Apart from its historic and agrarian landscapes, Lucena has a wide periphery that is the result of the normal processes of urban land extension which any city passing in four decades from approximately 28,000 to almost 43,000 inhabitants would experience. In addition, the situation has not been helped by the clear inability of the planning authorities to regulate development with an urban plan that would be in line with the new Andalusian law of urban planning, which modified the old subsidiary rules dating from 1989, and which, in turn, has followed the norm for delimitation of urban land since 1977, when expected growth was capped at scarcely more than ten per cent.[42]

As a result, the years which saw the greatest peak in building construction and public works were marked by no clear definition of urban planning control and an absolute disregard for the protection of the urban, agrarian and historical landscape. This has led to the current situation in which industrial, agrarian and residential lands are mixed

---

41   Inmaculada Caravaca et al., *Innovación y territorio*.

42   Javier Cabrera de la Colina, "Crecimiento urbano en ciudades pequeñas de las subbéticas centrales: Antequera y Lucena," in *La ciudad: tamaño y crecimiento – Coloquio de Geografía Urbana (1996)* (2005), 63–73.

Fig. 4: Transition zone with mixed uses between the industrial and the agrarian landscapes in El Pilar de la Dehesa, Lucena. Photo: Blanca Del Espino Hidalgo, 2012.

together in an apparent absence of regulatory measures and, in the process, has produced a soft and gradual transition between the urban and extra-urban landscape [Fig. 4].

5.2 Beja

Very close to the north-western Andalusian mountain ranges, the city of Beja possesses major relevance at a demographic level as well as acting as a functional centre for the territory of Baixo Alentejo, as it has done for centuries. This feature has favoured the confluence of two factors that mark its historic place in the great paradigm of the small cities in the southern part of the Peninsula: it has a rich heritage, although urban growth, derived from its enclave, has seen it relegated to a secondary position in terms of planning for its future development due to its location in the region of Alentejo. It is situated between the national N18 route from north to south and the N260 from west to east, and, in addition, is halfway between the important maritime port of Sines and the border with Spain in the area of Aracena.

Moreover, its proximity to the Spanish frontier area, with which there are not many major-quality link roads (in the southern half of Portugal, these tend to be mainly between Elvas and Badajoz, and between Algarve and the coast of Huelva), has led to its appearance on the agenda of the planning authorities as a strategic point at an infrastructural level.[43] This consideration, however, carries two important provisos: on the one hand, it means the construction of a passenger airport at the military air base which already exists in the north-west of the main urban core and, on the other – reinforcing the first – the building of a highway between the airport and the port of Sines, including a connection to one of the most important north-south axes of the country: the A2 highway.

The historic relevance of Beja from the Roman period onwards is a given. Although archaeological evidence exists of a settlement in the Iron Age, it was not until the foundation of the city of Pax Ilulia by the Emperor Augustus that Beja acquired a special importance in the territory. The capital of one of the three regions which composed the province of Lusitania, it was designated "civitas," namely the city responsible for the region's administration, as well as "colonia." Accordingly, it served as a focal point in the Roman governance of the territory, and was provided with important public spaces and monuments, of which only traces have continued to this day.[44] During the Visigoth period, a demographic decline began, and, since then, fluctuations in the role of Beja as a territorial centre have continued up until the 20th century, when the expansion of an urban periphery left a human vacuum in the central area.[45]

The ancient core of Beja is relatively small today in comparison with what is normally the case in other small cities, both Andalusian and Portuguese, with heritage traditions. As with Lucena, Beja's legacy is poorly protected and conserved, particularly if one takes into account the dimensions of its historic centre as well as the importance of the urban settlement itself through the centuries. Beja has sixteen elements classified and protected by official heritage laws, eight of which have the maximum degree of care (the castle, three churches, two monasteries, a civic building and a convent-hospital). Furthermore, five protection files were opened decades ago but not concluded satisfactorily, with three expired and two closed negatively. With regard to the less prominent heritage elements, the absence of an integral urban planning authority to deal with the historic areas of Beja, has led to the gradual obsolescence and consequent abandonment of traditional houses. All this suggests a poor standard of care and conservation for the historic urban landscape.

---

43   *Plan Regional de Ordenación del Territorio del Alentejo (PROTAlentejo)* (2010).

44   Abel Viana, *Origem e evolução histórica de Beja* (Beja: Minerva Comercial 1994).

45   Gabriel Mello de Mattos, "Uma planta de Beja no século XVI," *Arquivo de Beja*, Beja, vol. 1, fasc. III, 1944.

Fig. 5: Abandoned building in a noticeable state of degradation located in Praça da República, one of the public spaces with a major relevancy in the Historic Urban Landscape of Beja. Photo: Blanca Del Espino Hidalgo, 2013.

On top of that, efforts to protect valuable historic buildings do not extend to the urban fabric with regard to public spaces and its character as a unique ensemble [Picture 5]. This becomes particularly relevant if we examine the record of the planning authorities concerning the city in general and, more precisely, the centre of Beja: neither the Local Master Plan – revised in 2000 – nor the Special Plan for the Urbanisation of the Historic Core – published in 1986 and revised in 1995 – contains a catalogue of protected units or specific guidelines for the different homogeneous areas they include; rather they contain a double delimitation that corresponds to both a monumental area and a buffer zone.

The profusion of projects and development initiatives is, possibly, the other great distinguishing mark on the current urban and heritage management agenda. In fact, there is a strategy, promoted by the Local Chamber, to encourage cultural and economic activity as well as environmental initiatives, under the title "de Beja," which is publicised on the Internet through promotional videos and diverse projects that are in the pipeline. For the most part, this is geared towards providing incentives for investment in the different local productive sectors and,

Fig. 6: Beja Airport, surrounded by agricultural land.Photo: Blanca Del Espino Hidalgo, 2013.

in the hope of boosting entrepreneurial enterprise, attention is drawn to similar processes involving their Andalusian homologues. In this sense, the availability of land for building purposes in the industrial and tertiary sectors is featured along with encouragement for an ecological city, the creation of a research cluster, and the promotion of traditional agro-alimentary industries typical of the Mediterranean trilogy.

As a consequence, the large segments of agrarian landscape surrounding the city are systematically crossed by areas earmarked for economic growth. Among those, plans for a passenger airport [Picture 6], together with the abandoned, unconnected structural elements from the uncompleted highway, can be seen. At the same time, the transition landscape is interspersed with minor industrial installations and the historic centre is relegated to being the home of elder inhabitants and to sporadic sightseeing by tourists in a hierarchy of intentions and investments that have been re-located from outside to inside the city.

It seems clear that two problems have prevented the urban and infrastructural development of Beja from being accompanied by heritage, social and landscape revitalisation. There is, on the one hand, as already mentioned, the absence of an integral, strategic plan to unify efforts at promoting the various initiatives connected to the city's heritage and, on the other, an excessive emphasis on the development of emerging industries without considering traditional acumen, the agrarian landscape, heritage or even cultural tourism as major potential sources of equilibrium and sustainability.

6. Conclusions

Small cities in the southern part of the Iberian Peninsula are an ensemble of elements whose relevance as a case study requires progress in identification and the establishment of an academic corpus that would take their individual characteristics into account and not seek to assimilate them, in territorial or demographic terms, to other peninsular, European or worldwide equivalents. In this regard, a probable future research line concerning the definition of small cities might aim to recognise their networks as interconnected working sets, as well as to analyse them under their own particular conditions and contexts. At the same time, due consideration could be given to the relationships between the absolute centres, the intermediate centres and the capillary territorial terminals. In addition, more attention ought to be paid to understanding the regional perspective as a value to be reinforced and this, in turn, would help the cities find more balanced and sustainable conditions while working as an integrated whole.

In the context of a pause in growth and development rhythms, caused largely by an exceptionally critical socioeconomic situation, we have focused on a territorial fabric that has already been in receipt of vast investments in buildings and infrastructure. The belated recognition of a town's heritage as a possible profitable resource to enhance the cultural tourism industry, could, to some extent, palliate the effects of the abandonment suffered in recent periods as a result of a concentration on the development of urban structures and transport routes.

A focus on their heritage would probably stimulate the growth of the small cities themselves, as would the re-establishment of an identity based on their traditional crafts. Ignoring these issues poses a threat to the historic fabric that in the past created a balanced urban network. In order to achieve a more sustainable future for these settlements, it is essential to reflect on their current situation in a complex, far-ranging sense. This could start with an analysis of their recent history and take into account the strength of their heritage, the resources they were endowed with, and the errors that have led to their current crisis in urban, cultural and landscape terms. It will also be necessary to put in place, by means of the planning authorities and relevant legislation, the sensitive management of a territory that constitutes in itself a very valuable legacy.

Concluding remarks

Luďa Klusáková
and Marie-Vic Ozouf-Marignier

The focus of our volume has been on the strategies adopted by small towns to make themselves known, visible, and economically successful. The goal of the towns discussed has been to inform the outside world of their existence and their importance. Our chapters have explored a selection of cases from the second half of the twentieth and the beginning of the twenty-first century. Does a small number, a mere five chapters, dealing with disparate regional towns, deemed small in their respective countries, offer worthwhile findings and make a useful contribution to scholarly debate?

Urban history works with small numbers and with contrasting examples, so, too, does the history of architecture, art, urbanism, and urban sociology. A notable feature of such studies is that they generate questions which may turn into research topics. We think that this book will enrich an emerging interdisciplinary research area – heritage studies. The five chapters, each in its own way and using different spatial scales, posit their cases as representative of the European cultural heritage. Blanca Del Espino analysed small towns in the southern Spanish region of Andalusia and in Alentejo in the south of Portugal and adjusted her scale of reference to focus on two towns, one on either side of the national boundary. Tom Hulme and a team of British historians chose towns where historical pageants are staged, a practice that might be classified as an invented tradition. Martin Horáček brought the ideas and professional approach of an architect and art historian into play in his examination of the small town phenomenon in former Czechoslovakia. Two chapters concentrated on individual towns. Olga Moatsou looked in depth at the Cretan town of Rethymno against the backdrop of the Greek national context, while Greg Yudin and Yulia Koloshenko devoted their chapter to a single case study, that of the Russian town of Myshkin.

It is claimed in the introduction that small towns represent European urban culture, that they are culture makers and are themselves a product of that culture. While large towns are carriers of cosmopolitanism and the transnational transfer of new technologies, small towns have quite different priorities. For inhabitants, the recognized cultural heritage of their locale gives them the opportunity to build up identification with their small town and the surrounding region. Attachment to a larger entity, higher in hierarchy, is desirable and, ideally, a small town's heritage can transcend its immediate milieu and assume larger importance – regional, national, occasionally even global through the UNESCO world cultural heritage list. It might well be maintained that small towns are the carriers of the specificity as well as the diversity and variety of European culture through their urbanism, cohesive community life, and care for local cultural values. Uniqueness is often a means of linking local with national in monuments, architecture, the intangible heritage, and prominent personalities associated with a particular place. Just how significant these are is borne out in the case of Myshkin: when missing, they may be invented. Recently, under the influence of the tourist industry, it has become fashionable to label such a policy as branding. The city, the region, the nation, all are grouped together in order to "sell better." Regardless of our attitude towards this term borrowed from economic science, especially marketing, it shows that those who govern small towns are prepared to make the best of whatever is at hand – images and stereotypes whether based on actual or adapted fact, or even invention – to attract tourists, investors, and inhabitants. Small towns generate culture, each in its own unique way, and should be studied and analysed as carriers and promoters of European values.

Bibliography

Aguiar, José, Antonio Reis Cabrita and João Appleton. *Guião de apoio à reabilitação de edifícios habitacionais.* Lisbon: LNEC, 1998.

Allbaugh, Leland G. *Crete: A Case Study of an Underdeveloped Area.* Princeton, N.J.: University Press, 1953.

Almond, Gabriel A. and Sidney Verba. *The Civic Culture: Political Attitudes and Democracy in Five Nations.* London: Sage Publications, 1963.

Applegate, Celia. *A Nation of Provincials: The German Idea of Heimat.* Berkeley: University of California Press, 1990.

Argyropoulos, Thales. "I poleodomia kai i elliniki polis" [Town Planning and the Greek Town]. *Architektonika Themata* 1 (1967).

Arvanitakis, P. and Koutsoudakis, D. "Rythmistiki meleti Rethymnis kai touristikis anaptykseos ton akton tis" [Master Plan and Tourist Development of Rethymno]. *Architektonika Themata* 2 (1968).

Bakoš, Ján. *Discourses and Strategies: The Role of the Vienna School in Shaping Central European Approaches to Art History and Related Discourses.* Frankfurt am Main: Peter Lang, 2013.

Bakoš, Ján. *Intelektuál & pamiatka* [Intellectual & Monument]. Bratislava: Kalligram, 2004.

Balík, Stanislav. "Problematické institucionální stránky české místní samosprávy" [Problematic Institutional Issues of Czech Local Administration]. *Kontexty* 7, no. 5 (2015): 28–34. http://www.cdk.cz/casopisy/kontexty (accessed 15. 4. 2017).

Baumeister, Martin. "Die Hydra der Moderne. Masseneinwanderung und Wohnungspolitik in Madrid unter der Franco-Diktatur." *Informationen zur modernen Stadtgeschichte – Städte in Südeuropa* 1 (2009), 47–59. Berlin: Deutsches Institut für Urbanistik.

Beaven, Brad. *Visions of Empire: Patriotism, Popular Culture and the City, 1870–1939.* Manchester: Manchester University Press, 2012.

Beaven, Brad and John Griffiths. "Creating the exemplary citizen: The changing notion of citizenship in Britain 1870–1939." *Contemporary British History* 22 (2008), 203–225.

Beddow, Neil. *Turning Points: The Impact of Participation in Community Theatre.* Edited by Mary Schwartz. Bristol, n.d. [2001].

Beeton, Sue. *Community Development through Tourism.* Collingwood: Landlinks Press, 2006.

Begley, Siobhan. "Voluntary Associations and the Civic Ideal in Leicester, 1870–1939." PhD thesis, University of Leicester, 2009.

Bellet, Carmen and Josep Maria Llop, eds. *Ciudades intermedias y urbanización mundial.* Lleida: UNESCO, Ayuntament de Lleida, UIA, Ministerio de Asuntos Exteriores, 1999.

Bellet, Carmen and Josep Maria Llop. "Miradas a otros espacios urbanos: las ciudades intermedias." *Scripta Nova Geo Crítica, revista electrónica de geografía y ciencias sociales* 8, no. 165 (2004).

Boa, Elizabeth and Rachel Palfreyman. *Heimat: A German Dream.* Oxford: Oxford University Press, 2000.

Book of the Pageant, Greenwich. London: Fleetway, 1933.

Boorstin, Daniel J. *The Image: A Guide to Pseudo-Events in America.* New York: Harper, 1961.

Borrajo, Sebastián Justo. *La Ley de Carreteras y su reglamento.* Madrid: Dirección General de Carreteras, Ministerio de Fomento, 2006.

Borrmann, Norbert. *Paul Schultze-Naumburg 1869–1949: Maler – Publizist – Architekt.* Essen: Richard Bacht, 1989.

Bořutová, Dana. *Architekt Dušan Samuel Jurkovič.* Bratislava: Slovart, 2009.

Bouras, Charalambos, ed. *Eponyma archontika ton chronon tis Tourkokratias* [Distinguished Estates of the Ottoman Period]. Athens: NTUA Publications, 1986.

Brundtland, Gro Harlem, et al. *Brundtland Report. Our Common Future.* Oxford: Oxford University Press, 1987.

Burns, Arthur. "Beyond the 'Red Vicar': Community and Christian Socialism in Thaxted, Essex, 1910–1984." *History Workshop Journal* 75 (2013): 107.

Cabrera de la Colina, Javier. "Crecimiento urbano en ciudades pequeñas de las subbéticas centrales: Antequera y Lucena." In *La ciudad: tamaño y crecimiento – Coloquio de Geografía Urbana (1996)*, 2005. 63–73.

Capel, Horacio. "Ferrocarril, territorio y ciudades." *Revista Bibliográfica de Geografía y Ciencias Sociales* 12, no. 717 (2007).

Caravaca, Inmaculada, et al. *Innovación y Territorio. Análisis Comparado de Sistemas Productivos Locales en Andalucía.* Sevilla: Consejería de Economía y Hacienda, Colección Pablo de Olavide, Junta de Andalucía, 2002.

The Carlisle Pageant '77. Carlisle, 1977.

Chalmers, Roberts. "The Sherborne pageant." *The World's Work and Play* 6 (June 1905).

Chamberlin, Eric Russell. *The English Country Town*. Exeter: Webb & Bower, 1983.

Chandler, Jim A. *Explaining Local Government: Local Government in Britain Since 1800*. Manchester: Manchester University Press, 2007.

Clark, Peter, ed. *Small Towns in Early Modern Europe*. Cambridge: Cambridge University Press, 1995.

Cohen, Erich and Scott A. Cohen, "Current sociological theories and issues in tourism." *Annals of Tourism Research* 39, no. 4 (2012): 2177–2202.

Courtney, Paul and Andrew Errington. "The role of small towns in the local economy and some implications for development policy." *Local Economy* 15, no. 4 (2000): 280–301.

Crettaz-Stürzel, Elisabeth. *Heimatstil: Reformarchitektur in der Schweiz 1896–1914*. Frauenfeld – Stuttgart – Wien: Huber, 2005.

Crumley, Michele L. *Sowing Market Reforms: The Internationalization of Russian Agriculture*. New York: Palgrave Macmillan, 2013.

Davis, John. "Central government and the towns." In *Cambridge Urban History of Britain*, edited by Martin Daunton. Cambridge: Cambridge University Press, 2000. 261–286.

Dawson, Michael. "Party politics and the provincial press in early twentieth-century England." *Twentieth Century British History* 9 (1998): 201–218.

Dean, Joan FitzPatrick. *All Dressed Up: Modern Irish Historical Pageantry*. Syracuse, NY: Syracuse University Press, 2014.

Del Espino, Blanca et al. "Patrimonio, turismo e identidad en las ciudades medias del centro de Andalucía. Turismo en Andalucía y el norte de Marruecos: nuevos retos, nuevas propuestas." *ConecturMED*, Málaga, 2014.

Deligiannakis, Michalis. *Nomos Rethymnou, chorikes paremvaseis, nomothesia* [Municipality of Rethymno, Spatial Interventions, Regulations]. Rethymno: Kalaitzakis, 2005.

Díaz Quidiello, José Luis. "Las ciudades medias interiores en el Plan de Ordenación del Territorio de Andalucía." *Boletín PH*, no. 47 (2007): 44–53 Díaz Quidiello, José et al. *Atlas de la historia del territorio de Andalucía*. Sevilla: Instituto de Cartografía de Andalucía e Instituto Andaluz del Patrimonio Histórico, 2009.

Dickinson, Robert E. "The distribution and functions of the smaller urban settlements of East Anglia." *Geography* 17 (1932): 19–31.

Dilthey, Wilhelm. *Gesammelte Schriften, Bd. VI*. Leipzig: Teubner, 1924.

Dimakopoulos, Iordanis. *I katoikia sthn Kriti kata thn teleutaia periodo tis Enetokratias* [Housing in Crete during the Last Years of Venetocracy]. Athens: Goulandri – Chorn Foundation, 1997.

Dimakopoulos, Iordanis. "Ta spitia tou Rethemnou" [Houses of Rethymno]. Athens: *Dimosieumata tou archaiologikou deltiou*, no. 24, (1977).

Dimke, Daria and Irina Koryukhina. "Zavod po proizvodstvu vremeni" [A Time-production Factory]. *Otechestvennye Zapiski* 50, no. 5 (2012).

Dobson, Michael. *Shakespeare and Amateur Performance: A Cultural History.* Cambridge: Cambridge University Press, 2011.

Donovan, Victoria. "'Going backwards, we stride forwards:' Kraevedenie museums and the making of local memory in North West Russia, 1956–1981." *Forum for Anthropology and Culture* 7 (2012): 211–230.

Dostál, Oldřich, et al. *Československá historická města* [Czechoslovak Historic Towns and Cities]. Prague: Orbis, 1974.

Doxiadis, Constantinos A. "I Athina kai to mellon tis" [Athens and its Future]. *Architektoniki*, no. 26 (1961).

Doyle, Brian. "The invention of English." In *Englishness: Politics and Culture 1880–1920*, edited by Robert Colls and Philip Dodd. London: Croom Helm, 1986. 89–115.

Duany, Andres, Elizabeth Plater-Zyberk and Robert Alminana. *The New Civic Art: Elements of Town Planning.* New York: Rizzoli, 2003.

Duff, David. *The Life Story of H. R. H. Princess Louise, Duchess of Argyll.* London, 1949.

Engels, Friedrich. *La gens y el estado en Roma. El origen de la familia, la propiedad privada y el estado, VI.* Madrid: Alianza Editorial, 2008.

English, Jim. "Empire day in Britain, 1904–1958." *Historical Journal* 49 (2006): 247–276.

"Eparhiaki Ellas" [Provincial Greece]. *Kritiki Epitheorisi* (7 February 1960).

"Ergostasio tsimenton me imerisia paragogi 1,500 tonnon tha idrythi sto Irakleion" [A Cement Plant with a Daily Production of 1,500 Tons Will Be Founded in Heraklion]. *Rethemniotika Nea* (4 December 1966).

Esty, Jed. *A Shrinking Island: Modernism and National Culture in England.* Princeton and Oxford: Princeton University Press, 2004.

Ewen, Shane. "Power and administration in two Midland cities." PhD thesis, University of Leicester 2003.

Feria Toribio, José M., et al. *El sistema urbano andaluz. Aglomeraciones urbanas, áreas de centralidad y ámbitos desarticulados.* Sevilla: Instituto de Desarrollo Regional, Consejería de Obras Públicas y Transportes, 1992.

Ferrao, João. "Rede urbana portuguesa: uma visão internacional." Janus (2011), 52–57.

Fernández Cacho, Silvia, et al. *Paisajes y patrimonio cultural en Andalucía. Tiempo, usos e imágenes.* 2 vol., PH cuadernos, no. 27. Sevilla: Junta de Andalucía, Instituto Andaluz del Patrimonio Histórico, 2010.

Fernández Salinas, Víctor. "Paisaje urbano en las ciudades medias." *Boletín PH*, no. 63 (2007): 54–61.

Fragner, Benjamin. "Druhá zpráva o Urbanitě" [Second Report about the Urbanita Exhibition]. *Technický magazín* 32, no. 1 (1989): 6–11.

Fraser, Derek. *The Evolution of the British Welfare State: A History of Social Policy since the Industrial Revolution*. Basingstoke, 2009.

Freeman, Mark. "'Splendid display, pompous spectacle:' Historical pageants in twentieth-century Britain." *Social History* 38 (2013): 423–455.

Freeman, Mark. *St Albans: A History*. Lancaster: Carnegie Publishing, 2008.

Fryganakis, Yorgos. *I Rethemniotiki pena kai oi prosfyges tis Mikrasiatikis katastrofis* [The Rethemniot Pen and the Refugees of the Asia Minor Catastrophe]. Rethymne: Rethemnos newspaper, 2011.

Gasser, Manuel. "Wanderungen auf Kreta, Feriennotizen von M. G." *Weltwoche*, no. 1227 (17 May 1957).

Glassberg, David. *American Historical Pageantry*. Chapel Hill, NC: University of North Carolina Press, 1990.

Gliddon, Paul. "The political importance of provincial newspapers, 1903–1945: The Rowntrees and the liberal press." *Twentieth Century British History* 14 (2003): 24–42.

Goodden, Cecil P. *The Story of the Sherborne Pageant*. Sherborne, 1906.

Gorsky, Martin. "Public health in interwar England and Wales: Did it fail?" *Dynamis* 28 (2008): 175–198.

Gullace, Nicoletta F. *"The Blood of Our Sons": Men, Women and the Renegotiation of British Citizenship during the Great War*. Basingstoke, 2002.

Gunn, Simon. *The Public Culture of the Victorian Middle Class*. Manchester: Manchester University Press, 2000.

Gutkind, Erwin A. "Urban development in East-Central Europe: Poland, Czechoslovakia, and Hungary." *International History of City Development* 7, with contributions by Wojciech Kalinowski, Members of the Union of Architects of the Czechoslovak Socialist Republic, and Imre Perényi, edited by Gabriele Gutkind, New York: The Free Press; London: Collier-Macmillan, 1972.

Haas, Tigran, ed. *New Urbanism and Beyond: Designing Cities for the Future*. New York: Rizzoli, 2008.

Hajkowski, Thomas. *The BBC and National Identity in Britain 1922–1953*. Manchester: Manchester University Press, 2010.

Hannigan, John. *Fantasy City*. London: Taylor & Francis, 1998.

Harry Mottram. "The Axbridge Pageant." *Somerset Magazine* 10, no. 8 (August 2000).

Hayes, Nick. "Civic perceptions: Housing and local decision-making in English cities in the 1920s." *Urban History* 27 (2000): 211–233.

Hayes, Nick. "Counting civil society: Deconstruction elite participation in the provincial English city, 1900–1950." *Urban History* 40 (2013): 287–314.

Hendley, Matthew C. *Organized Patriotism and the Crucible of War: Popular Imperialism in Britain, 1914–1932*. Montreal: McGill-Queen's University Press, 2012.

Herzfeld, Michael. *A Place in History: Social and Monumental Time in a Cretan Town*. Princeton, N.J.: Princeton University Press, 1991.

Hobsbawm, Eric and Terence Ranger. *The Invention of Tradition*. Cambridge: Cambridge University Press, 1992.

Hofer, Sigrid. *Reformarchitektur 1900–1918: Deutsche Baukünstler auf der Suche nach dem nationalen Stil*. Stuttgart – London: Edition Axel Menges, 2005.

Horáček, Martin. "Architekt Jan Vejrych ve Slaném, reformovaná česká renesance a velké stavby na malém českém městě" [The Architect Jan Vejrych in Slaný, the Reformed Czech Renaissance and Large Buildings in a Small Czech Town]. In *Od kabaly k Titaniku: Deset studií nejen z dějin umění* [From Kabbalah to Titanic: Ten Studies in Art History], edited by Lubomír Konečný et al. Prague: Artefactum, 2013. 69–101.

Horáček, Martin. *Za krásnější svět: Tradicionalismus v architektuře 20. a 21. století* [Toward a More Beautiful World: Traditionalism in Architecture of the 20th and 21st Centuries]. Brno: Barrister & Principal – VUTIUM, 2013.

Howard, Ebenezer. *To-morrow: A Peaceful Path to Real Reform*. London: Swan Sonnenschein & Co, 1898.

Hulme, Tom. "Civic culture and citizenship: The nature of urban governance in interwar Manchester and Chicago." PhD thesis, University of Leicester, 2013.

Husserl, Edmund. *Ideas for a Pure Phenomenology and Phenomenological Philosophy: First Book*. Dordrecht: Kluwer, 1998.

Husserl, Edmund. *Phantasy, Image Consciousness, and Memory*. Dordrecht: Kluwer, 2005.

Ironside Wood, Olga. *Edmund of Anglia*. Bury St Edmunds: Souvenir programme. Festival of St Edmund [Bury Free Press supplement], 1970.

Jacobs, Jane. *The Death and Life of Great American Cities*. New York: Random House, 1961 [Czech edition 1975].

Judge, Roy. "Merrie England and the Morris 1881–1910." *Folklore* 104 (1993): 124–143.

Kaklamanis, Stefanos, Mauromatis Yiannis and Vasias Tsokopoulos. *Candia / Creta / Kriti – O choros kai o chromos: 16os–18os aionas* [Candia / Creta / Crete – Space and Time: 16th–17th Centuries]. Athens: National Bank Cultural Foundation, 2005.

Kalitsounakis, Ioannis. "Entyposeis Elvetou periigitou apo tin Kriti" [Impressions of Crete of a Swiss Traveller]. *Kritiki Protochronia* 3 (1963).

Kalogeras, Nikos. "I astiki polykatoikia kai i synecheia tou modernismou stin Ellada" [The Urban Polykatoikia and the Resumption of Modernism in Greece], *Design + Art in Greece* 29 (1998), 36–46.

Kayser, Bernard. *La renaissance rurale. Sociologie des campagnes du monde occidental.* Paris: Armand Colin, 1990.

Kern, Stephen. *The Culture of Time and Space 1880–1918.* Cambridge, MA: Harvard University Press, 2003.

Kibic, Karel and Aleš Vošahlík. *Památková ochrana a regenerace historických měst v České republice 1945–2010* [Heritage Protection and Renovation of Historical Towns of the Czech Republic 1945–2010]. Prague: Národní památkový ústav, 2011.

Kritiki Epitheorisi (17 July 1977).

Koss, Stephen. *The Rise and Fall of the Political Press in Britain. Volume II: The Twentieth Century.* London: Hamish Hamilton, 1984.

Kroha, Jiří. "Doslov: Socialistická vazba městských sídel se životním prostředím" [Afterword: The Communist Connection between Cities and the Environment, 1965]. In Bohuslav Fuchs. *Nové zónování – urbanistická tvorba životního prostředí z hlediska sídelního a krajinného* [New Zoning – Urban Planning of the Environment from the Standpoint of Sites and Landscape]. Prague: Academia, 1967. 84–95.

Kühn, Manfred. "Small towns in rural areas – What are the possibilities in the periphery?" *Peripheral Small Towns, IRS Aktuell, Newsletter for Social Science-Based Spatial Research* 6 (September 2014): 1–13.

Lappo, Georgij M. *Goroda Rossii: Vzgliad geografa* [Russian Cities: A Geographer's View]. Moscow: Novyi khronograf, 2012.

Lawrence, Jon. *Speaking for the People: Party, Language and Popular Politics in England, 1867–1914.* Cambridge: Cambridge University Press, 1998.

Lawrence, Jon and Miles Taylor. "Introduction: Electoral sociology and the historians." In *Party, State, and Society: Electoral Behaviour in Britain since 1820*, edited by Lawrence Jon and Taylor Miles. Aldershot: Scolar Press, 1997. 1–26.

van Leeuwen, Eveline S. *Urban-Rural Interactions. Towns as Focus Points in Rural Development, Contributions to Economics.* Berlin – Heidelberg: Physica Verlag, 2010.

Legg, Rodney. *The Book of Bridport: Town, Harbour and West Bay.* Bath – Tiverton: Halsgrove, 2003.

Lentisco, David. *Cuando el hierro se hace camino, historia del ferrocarril en España.* Madrid: Alianza Editorial, 2005.

Lorenc, Vilém, et al. *Rekonstrukce historických měst* [Reconstruction of Historical Towns]. Prague: SÚRPMO, 1956.

Lovell, Hilda. "Axbridge, Somerset: History of a Domesday Borough with special reference to the development of local government." MPhil thesis, University of London, 1971.

MacCannell, Dean. "Staged authenticity: Arrangements of social space in tourist settings." *American Journal of Sociology* 79, no. 3 (1973), 589–603.

Macharáčková, Marcela, ed. *Jiří Kroha (1893–1974): Architect, Painter, Designer, Theorist: A 20th-Century Metamorphosis.* Brno: Muzeum města Brna, 2007.

Maloutas, Thomas. "Athens before the socio-demographic challenges in the beginning of the 21st century." In *2010 Hamburg, La Fabrique de la Cité (Groupe VINCI).* Proceedings of the conference The City is Alive, Hamburg, 2010.

Manuel do Carmo, Ricardo. "Cidades médias. Do crescimento demográfico à consolidação territorial." *Cidades – Comunidades e Territórios,* no. 12/13 (2006): 69–82.

Marques, Teresa Sá, et al. *Sistema Urbano Nacional. Cidades médias e dinâmicas territoriais.* 2 vol. Lisbon: Direcção-Geral do Ordenamento do Território e Desenvolvimento Urbano, 1997.

Marques da Costa, Eduarda. "Uma nota sobre as políticas das cidades em Portugal nos anos noventa." *Inforgeo* 14, Lisbon: Edições Colibri 1999. 131–137.

Mavromatis, I. E. *Oikonomia tis Kritis 1951–1981.* Vol. A [The Economy of Crete 1951–1981]. Heraklio, 1989.

Mello de Mattos, Gabriel. "Uma planta de Beja no século XVI." *Arquivo de Beja,* vol. 1, fasc. III, Beja, 1944.

Mitscherlich, Alexander. *Die Unwirtlichkeit unserer Städte: Anstiftung zum Unfrieden.* Frankfurt am Main: Suhrkamp, 1965 [Slovak edition 1971].

Moatsou, Olga. "Polykatoikia, 1960–2000: Entrepreneurial housing, from Athens to Rethymno." PhD thesis, Lausanne: École polytechnique fédérale de Lausanne (EPFL), 2014.

Moutsopoulos, Nikos. *I architektoniki proeksochi (to sachnisi). Symvoli sti meleti tou ellinikou spitiou* [The Bay Window (şahniş): A Contribution to the Study of the Greek House]. Thessaloniki: Society for Macedonian Studies, 1988.

Nathan, Matthew. *The Annals of West Coker.* Cambridge: Cambridge University Press, 1957.

Nelles, Henri V. *The Art of Nation-Building: Pageantry and Spectacle at Quebec's Tercentenary.* Toronto: University of Toronto Press, 1999.

Nicholas, Sian. "From John Bull to John Citizen: Images of national identity and citizenship on the wartime BBC." In *The Right to Belong: Citizenship and National Identity in Britain, 1930–1960,* edited by Richard Weight – Abigail Beach, London: I. B. Tauris 1998. 36–58.

The Pageant of Buxton in Light and Sound. London, 1958.

The Pageant of Newark: Official Programme. Newark, 1936.

Pageant of Parliament. London, 1934.

Palmowski, Jan. *Inventing a Socialist Nation: Heimat and the Politics of Everyday Life in the GDR, 1945–1990.* Cambridge: Cambridge University Press, 2009.

Parry, Jonathan. "Whig monarchy, whig nation: Crown, politics and representativeness 1800–2000." In *The Monarchy and the British Nation 1780 to the Present*, edited by Andrzej Olechnowicz. Cambridge: Cambridge University Press, 2007. 47–75.

Pérez Azaustre, Joaquín. *Lucena sefardita: la ciudad de los poetas.* Barcelona: Andalucía Abierta, 2005.

Rampley, Matthew. *The Vienna School of Art History: Empire and the Politics of Scholarship, 1847–1918.* University Park: Penn State University Press, 2013.

Readman, Paul. "The place of the past in English culture c. 1890–1914." *Past and Present* 186 (2005): 147–199.

Redcliffe-Maud, John P. R. and Bruce Wood. *English Local Government Reformed.* London: Oxford University Press, 1974.

Reese, Laura A. and Raymond A. Rosenfeld. "Comparative civic culture: theory and methods." In *Comparative Civic Culture: The Role of Local Culture in Urban Policy-Making*, edited by Laura A. Reese and Raymond A. Rosenfeld. Farnham: Ashgate Publishing Limited, 2012. 3–20.

"Research in urban history." *Urban History* 2 (1975): 54–188.

Rethemniotis (pen-name). "Rethemniotikes kouventes." [Rethemniot Conversations] *Kritiki Epitheorisi* (25 January 1969).

Richards, Alexandra. *Slow Dorset: Local, Characterful Guides to Britain's Special Places.* Chalfont St Peter: Bradt, 2012.

Richards, Greg and Derek Hall. "The community: A sustainable concept in tourism development?" In *Tourism and Sustainable Community Development*, edited by Derek Hall – Greg Richards. London: Sage, 2000. 1–14.

Ritzer, George and Allan Liska. "McDisneyization and 'post-tourism': Complementary perspectives on contemporary tourism." In *Touring Cultures: Transformations of Travel and Theory*, edited by Chris Rojek and Urry John. London – New York: Taylor & Francis, 2003. 96–111.

Rivas Carmona, Jesús. *Arquitectura barroca cordobesa.* Córdoba: Monte de Piedad y Caja de Ahorros de Córdoba, 1982.

Rodrick, Anne B. *Self-Help and Civic Culture: Citizenship in Victorian Birmingham.* Ashgate, 2004.

Roháček, Jiří and Kristina Uhlíková, eds. *Zdeněk Wirth pohledem dnešní doby* [Zdeněk Wirth in Contemporary View]. Prague: Artefactum, 2010.

Romsey Millenary Celebration A.D. 907–A.D. 1907: Words and Music. Romsey, 1907.

Royle, Stephen A. "The development of small towns in Britain." In *Cambridge Urban History of Britain: Volume III*, edited by Martin Daunton. Cambridge: Cambridge University Press, 2000. 151–184.

Samuel, Raphael. *Theatres of Memory. Volume I: Past and Present in Contemporary Culture*. London: Verso, 1994.

Santos, Jorge A. "Problemas fundamentais do tráfego e dos transportes em Portugal. Questões estratégicas." *Análise Psicológica* 13, no. 3 (1995): 249–252.

Schultze-Naumburg, Paul. *Kulturarbeiten I–IX*. München: Kunstwart, 1901–1917.

Semsroth, Klaus, Kari Jormakka, and Bernhard Langer, eds. *Kunst des Städtebaus: Neue Perspektiven auf Camillo Sitte*. Wien – Köln – Weimar: Böhlau, 2005.

Shapely, Peter. *The Politics of Housing: Power, Consumers and Urban Culture*. Manchester, Manchester University Press, 2007.

Simmel, Georg. "The metropolis and mental life." In *The Blackwell City Reader*, edited by Gary Bridge – Sophie Watson. Chichester: Wiley-Blackwell, 2010. 103–110.

Sitte, Camillo. *Der Städte-Bau nach seinen künstlerischen Grundsätzen*. Wien: Carl Graeser & Co., 1901.

Šlapeta, Vladimír, ed. *Jan Kotěra, 1871–1923: The Founder of Modern Czech Architecture*. Prague: Kant, 2003.

St Albans and its Pageant. St Albans: Smith's printing agency, 1907.

Stapleton, Julia. "Citizenship versus Patriotism in Twentieth-Century England." *Historical Journal* 48 (2005): 151–178.

Statham, Margaret. *The Book of Bury St Edmunds*. Buckingham, England: Barracuda books, 1988.

Steiner, Carol and Yvette Reisinger. "Understanding Existential Authenticity." *Annals of Tourism Research* 33, no. 2 (2006): 299–318.

Stern, Robert A. M., Fishman, David and Tilove, Jacob. *Paradise Planned: The Garden Suburb and the Modern City*. New York: The Monacelli Press, 2013.

Street, John. "Political culture – from civic culture to mass culture." *British Journal of Political Science* 24 (1994): 95–113.

Sugg Ryan, Deborah "'Pageantitis': Frank Lascelles' 1907 Oxford historical pageant, Visual spectacle and popular memory." *Visual Culture in Britain* 8 (2007): 63–82.

Tanner, Duncan. "The Labour Party and electoral politics in the coalfields." In *Miners, Unions, and Politics, 1910–47*, edited by Alan Campbell, Nina Fishman and David Howell. Aldershot: Scolar Press, 1996. 59–92.

Tanner, Duncan. *Political Change and the Labour Party 1900–1918*. Cambridge: Cambridge University Press, 1990.

The Thirsk Historical Play. Thirsk, 1907.

Trainor, Richard H. "The 'decline' of British urban governance since 1850: A reassessment." In *Urban Governance: Britain and Beyond since 1750*, edited by Robert J. Morris and Richard H. Trainor. Aldershot: Ashgate, 2000. 28–46.

Twinch, Carol. *Bury St Edmunds: A History and Celebration*. Salisbury, 2004.

Uhlíková, Kristina. *Zdeněk Wirth, první dvě životní etapy (1878–1939)* [First Two Stages of Life of Zdeněk Wirth (1878–1939)]. Prague: Národní památkový ústav, 2010.

Urry, John. *The Tourist Gaze.* London: SAGE, 2002.

Vaitsos, Kostis and Giannitsis Tasos. *Technologikos metaschimatismos kai oikonomiki anaptyksi* [Technological Transformation and Economic Growth]. Athens: Gutenberg, 1987.

Viana, Abel. *Origem e evolução histórica de Beja.* Beja: Minerva Comercial, 1994.

Viciano Joan et al. "A Probable Case of Gigantism/Acromegaly in Skeletal Remains from the Jewish Necrópolis of 'Ronda Sur' (Lucena, Córdoba, Spain; VIII–XII Centuries CE)." *Antropologischer Anzeiger* 71, no. 1 (2015): 67–87.

Vlnas, Vít. "Od šestky k trojkám" [From the Six to the Troikas]. In *Proměny dějin umění: Akta druhého sjezdu historiků umění*, edited by Roman Prahl – Tomáš Winter. Dolní Břežany: Scriptorium, 2007. 201–208.

Wallis, Mick. "The popular front pageant: Its emergence and decline." *New Theatre Quarterly* 11 (1996): 17–32.

Wang, Ning. "Rethinking authenticity in tourism experience." *Annals of Tourism Research* 26, no. 2 (1999): 349–370.

Weight, Richard and Abigail Beach. "Introduction." In *The Right to Belong: Citizenship and National Identity in Britain, 1930–1960*, edited by Richard Weight and Abigail Beach. London: I. B. Tauris, 1998. 1–18.

White, Jerry. "From Herbert Morrison to command and control: The decline of local democracy and its effect on public services." *History Workshop Journal* 59 (2005): 73–82.

Wildman, Charlotte. "Urban transformation in Liverpool and Manchester, 1918–1939." *Historical Journal* 55 (2012): 119–143.

Wildman, William B. *A Short History of Sherborne from 705 AD.* Sherborne, 1896.

Winter, Jay M. "British national identity and the First World War." In *The Boundaries of the State in Modern Britain*, edited by S. J. D. Green – Richard C. Whiting. Cambridge: Cambridge University Press, 2002. 261–277.

Wirth, Zdeněk. "Selský dům" [Rural House]. *Stavitel* 2, no. 11–12 (1920–1921): 141–148.

Wirth, Zdeněk. "Stavební rhytmus malého města" [The Architectural Rhythm of a Small Town]. *Styl* 1 (1909): 327–336.

Woods, Michael. "Performing power: Local politics and the Taunton pageant of 1928." *Journal of Historical Geography* 25 (1999): 57–74.

Yoshino, Ayako. "'Between the acts' and Louis Napoleon Parker – the creator of the modern English pageant." *Critical Survey* 15, no. 2 (2003): 49–60.

Yoshino, Ayako. *Pageant Fever: Local History and Consumerism in Edwardian England.* Tokyo, 2011.

Zarecor, Kimberly Elman. *Manufacturing a Socialist Modernity: Housing in Czecho-slovakia 1945–1960.* Pittsburgh: University of Pittsburgh Press, 2011.

Zemło, Mariusz. "Tradycjonalizm małego miasta." In *Małe Miasta. Historia i współczesność,* ["Small Town's Traditionalism". In *Small Towns. History and Present Times*]. Edited by Mariusz Zemło and Przemysław Czyżewski. Supraśl, 2001.

Official documents and laws

Despachos of the MPAT 6/94 and 7/94 (PROSIURB), Lisbon: Government of Portugal, 1994.

Despacho of the MAOT 47/A/99 (POLIS), Government of Portugal, 1999.

European Landscape Convention, Florence: Council of Europe, 2010.

Plan de Ordenación Territorial de Andalucía (POTA), Seville: Government of Andalusia, 2006.

Plan Regional de Ordenación del Territorio del Algarve (PROTAlgarve), Lisbon: Government of Portugal, 2007.

Plan Regional de Ordenación del Territorio del Alentejo (PROTAlentejo), Lisbon: Government of Portugal, 2010.

Archival Sources

Bridport Royal Charter Pageant 1253–1953. Dorset History Centre, D.2089/5.

Highlights from the History of an Ancient Royal Borough Presented by the People of Axbridge and District. Somerset Heritage Centre, PAM 89.

"Newark Pageant." *Newark Pageant Minute Book.* Nottingham Archive, DD/NM/15/15/1.

The Sherborne Pageant: Full Report of the Preliminary Meeting, held in the Digby Assembly Rooms, on Thursday, July 14th, 1904. (Sherborne 1904), Dorset History Centre, PE/SH: PA1/1.

Sherborne Pageant: An Unique Historical Spectacle or Folk Play (Sherborne 1905), Dorset History Centre, PE/SH: PA2/3-2/4.

St. Aldhelm Celebration: The "Daily Mail." Interview with Mr. Louis Parker. Dorset History Centre, PE/SH: PA3/1.

Statement of Accounts Balance Sheet: Auditor's Report and Certificate. File of correspondence with the Pageant organisers; *Application of F. T. Carter to be Pageant Secretary*; papers and correspondence relating to the disposal of surplus funds (1907), Suffolk Record Office, Bury St Edmunds branch, EE500/34/1.

Electronic sources

The Axbridge Pageant. http://www.axbridgepageant.org.uk/.

Eardley, Alison, ed. *Small Towns of the Future, Not the Past.* Essay no. 1 (September 2011), http://www.smalltownsfortomorrow.org/wp-content/uploads /2011/07/STfT-Essay1-WEB.pdf (accessed 19. 4. 2017).

European Council for the Village and Small Town. http://www.ecovast.org/english /index%20.htm. (accessed 28. 10.2016).

The European Association of Historic Towns and Regions. http://www.historic-towns. org/ (accessed 26. 10. 2016).

Eurostat, statistics (accessed 16. 9. 2016). http://ec.europa.eu/eurostat/cache/RSI /#?vis=city.statistics&lang=en.

Eurostat, urban typology (accessed 16. 9. 2016). http://ec.europa.eu/eurostat/cache /RSI/#?vis=typologies.urb_typology&lang=en.

Houillon, Vincent – Laurence Thomsin. "Définitions du rural et de l'urbain dans quelques pays européens." *Espace, populations, sociétés. Repopulation et mobilités rurales.* (1 February 2001), 195–200. http://www.persee.fr/web/revues/home/ prescript/article/espos_0755-7809_2001_num_19_1_1989 (accessed 15. 4. 2017).

International Association of Peace Messenger Cities http://www.iapmc.org/cities.aspx (accessed 3. 3. 2012).

The International Cities of Peace Organization http://www.internationalcitiesof peace.org/what/what.html (accessed 3. 3. 2012).

Kayser, Bernard. "Les citadins au village." *Espace, populations, sociétés. Repopulation et mobilités Rurales.* (1 February2001), 151–160. http://www.persee.fr/web /revues/home/prescript/article/espos_0755-7809_2001_num_19_1_1983 (accessed 15. 4. 2017).

Mafalda Rodrigues, Ana. *Regulação urbanística e forma da nova expansão urbana: o caso de Évora.* Universidade de Coimbra, Coimbra 2006. http://hdl.handle.net /10316/6003 (accessed 24. 9. 2014).

Morris, Gordon. *Small Towns, Big Societies.* Essay no. 2 (November 2011). http:// www.smalltownsfortomorrow.org/wp-content/uploads/2011/10/STfT_ Essay2_WEB.pdf (accessed 19. 4. 2017).

The Redress of the Past: Historical Pageants in Britain, 1905–2016. http://www. historicalpageants.ac.uk (accessed 19. 4. 2017).

Rojas, Andrés, "Las ciudades medias y la expansión territorial," *La Ciudad Viva.* [Online]. Friday, 23rd October 2009. http://www.laciudadviva.org/blogs /?p=2895 (accessed 1. 7. 2014).

Sdružení historických sídel Čech, Moravy a Slezska (SHS ČMS). http://www.historicka-sidla.cz/ (accessed 26. 10. 2016).

Svaz měst a obcí České republiky (SMO ČR). http://www.smocr.cz/cz/svaz-mest-a-obci-cr/kdo-jsme/kdo-jsme.aspx (accessed 26. 10. 2016).

The Council of European Municipalities and Regions. http://www.ccre.org/en (accessed 4. 4. 2017).

United Cities and Local Governments (UCLG). http://www.cities-localgovernments.org/sections.asp (accessed 3. 3. 2012).

Vision of Britain. http://www.visionofbritain.org.uk/ (accessed 19. 4. 2017).

World Union of Cities for Peace (WUCP). http://www.uia.org/s/or/en/1100046107 (accessed 4. 4. 2017).

Združenie miest a obcí Slovenska. http://www.zmos.sk/ (accessed 26. 10. 2016).

Zgrajová Lenka. *Svaz měst a obcí očima století.* http://smocr.cz/o-svazu/z-historie/koreny-svazu.aspx (accessed 26. 10. 2016).

Związek Miast Polskich. http://www.zmp.poznan.pl/strona-22-historia.html (accessed 26. 10. 2016).

Note on Authors

Angela Bartie is a Lecturer in Scottish History in the School of History, Classics and Archaeology at the University of Edinburgh, and a co-investigator on the AHRC-funded project "The Redress of the Past: Historical Pageants in Britain, 1905–2016" (award number AH/K003887/1). Her main research interests focus on cultural and social change in modern (post-1940) Scotland, with specific interests in the role of the arts in society, cultural policy, and arts festivals. These were explored in her book, *The Edinburgh Festivals: Culture and Society in Post-war Britain*, Edinburgh 2013.

Linda Fleming is a Research Associate in Economic and Social History in the School of Social and Political Sciences at the University of Glasgow, and a researcher on the AHRC-funded project "The Redress of the Past: Historical Pageants in Britain, 1905–2016" (award number AH/K003887/1). Her research ranges widely across the social and cultural history of modern Scotland, concentrating particularly on the history of communities, and how the past informs perceptions of these in the present. She recently co-edited *Scottish Women: a Documentary History, 1780–1914*, Edinburgh 2013.

Mark Freeman is a Reader in Education and Social History in the Department of Education, Practice and Society at the UCL Institute of Education, University College London, and a co-investigator on the AHRC-funded project "The Redress of the Past: Historical Pageants in Britain, 1905–2016" (award number AH/K003887/1). He specialises in modern British social and educational history, and has published widely on topics such as the Joseph Rowntree Charitable Trust, historical pageants, Quakerism, and the history of St Albans. He is a co-editor of the journal *History of Education*. His latest co-authored book was *Shareholder*

Democracies? Corporate Governance in Britain and Ireland before 1850 ,Chicago 2012.

Blanca Del Espino Hidalgo is a Doctor in Architecture. She works as a Doctoral Assistant at the University of Seville, Urban and Land Planning Department, and at the History, Theory and Composition in Architecture Department. She earned a Master's in Architecture and Cultural Heritage and a Master's in Sustainable City and Architecture. She has developed a research line about sustainability in urban heritage, especially concerning small cities in the inner lands of Andalusia, as well as the case of the small cities in the southern regions of Portugal. She is in charge of the Coordination of the Second Strategic Plan of the city of Lucena (Andalusia), where she deals with sustainable integrated urban development and citizen participation mechanisms regarding urban heritage.

Martin Horáček is an Associate Professor of Art and Architectural History, Theory, and Heritage Conservation at the Faculty of Architecture, Brno University of Technology, and the Department of Art Education of the Palacký University of Olomouc. He is an author of three books, among them *Za krásnější svět. Tradicionalismus v architektuře 20. a 21. století* [Toward a More Beautiful World: Traditionalism in Architecture of the 20th and 21st Centuries] Brno 2013 (in Czech with an extensive English summary), and co-author of the monographs: *Great Villas of Bohemia, Moravia and Silesia*, Prague 2010; *Naprej! Czech Sports Architecture 1567–2012*, Prague 2012; and, *Revival: Memories, Identities, Utopias*, London 2015.

Tom Hulme is a Lecturer in Modern British History in the School of History, Anthropology, Philosophy and Politics at Queen's University Belfast, and a former researcher on the AHRC-funded project "The Redress of the Past: Historical Pageants in Britain, 1905–2016" (award number AH/K003887/1). He specialises in twentieth-century British and American urban history, and is particularly interested in questions of citizenship and community in the 1920s and 1930s. His first monograph, provisionally titled *After the Shock City: Manchester, Chicago and the Making of the Modern Citizen, 1918–1939*, is under contract with the Royal Historical Society Studies in History series.

Luďa Klusáková is full Professor of History, chair of the Seminar of General and Comparative History at the Faculty of Arts at Charles University in Prague. She took her scientific degree from the same university in 1981 for her comparative research on the modernization of European urban networks. Later she researched on the problems of perception of space, urban innovations, collective identities, modernity and backwardness. Published, edited and co-edited twelve international collective books mostly in English on these problems. Her current interest in the role of history in the creation of regional and urban identities is a continuation of "Between urban and rural culture: Public use of history and cultural heritage in building collective identities (1990–2007)," in Klusáková, Luďa – Teulières, Laure (eds). *Frontiers and Identities. Cities in Regions and Nations*. Pisa: Edizioni Plus Pisa University Publisher 2008, 299–322.

Yulia Koloshenko is a graduate student in sociology at the University of Manchester and the Moscow School of Social and Economic Sciences and a research fellow at St. Tikhon's Orthodox University. Her research interests are feminist studies and the sociology of communities.

Olga Moatsou received her diploma in architecture at the National Technical University of Athens in 2005, and a Master of Advanced Studies at the ETH in Zurich in 2006. From 2004 to 2009 she worked as an architect in Zurich and Athens. She then did her doctoral thesis at the Swiss Federal Institute of Technology in Lausanne, which she completed in the beginning of 2014 under the direction of Professor Bruno Marchand. The thesis' title was "Polykatoikia, 1960–2000. Entrepreneurial housing, from Athens to Rethymno" and treated matters of housing typologies, agents' roles in housing production, welfare practices in remote areas and bottom-up urban growth. She is currently working at the Swiss Society of Engineers and Architects in Zurich, but her passion for history, housing and urbanity keep her active in the field of academia through publications, meetings and conferences.

Marie-Vic Ozouf-Marignier is a historian and geographer, and is a Director of Studies at EHESS. She is in charge of the "Territoires, espaces, societies" master's programme and the "Territoires, sociétés, développement" doctoral programme. A specialist in the methods of dividing and representing territory she runs a seminar on "Infra-state territorial decentralisation and reorganisation, identities, development know-how." She has published: La formation des départements, Ed. de l'EHESS, 1992, Atlas de la Révolution française, Ed. de l'EHESS, 1989, and Géographes en pratiques, Presses universitaires de Rennes, 2001.

She regularly takes part in European programmes, in particular with Hungary, Italy and Spain.

Paul Readman is a Professor in Modern British History in the Department of History, and a Vice-Dean for Research, at King's College London, and the principal investigator on the AHRC-funded project "The Redress of the Past: Historical Pageants in Britain, 1905–2016" (award number AH/K003887/1). His research interests lie in modern British political and cultural history, including electoral and agrarian politics, landscape preservation, the politics of patriotism, foreign policy, historiography and historical methods, and the place of the past in late Victorian and Edwardian culture. His most recent co-edited book was *Walking Histories, 1800–1914*, Basingstoke: Palgrave Macmillan 2016.

Greg Yudin is a senior researcher at the Laboratory for Studies in Economic Sociology and a senior lecturer at the Department of Social Sciences at the National Research University –Higher School of Economics in Moscow. He earned a double MA in Sociology from the University of Manchester and the Higher School of Economics, and a PhD in Philosophy from the Higher School of Economics. His research interests are political theory and the phenomenology of the social world, and his work focuses on the cognitive and technological foundations of the economy.